The Rose of Baghdad

Mathew Carter

It is my sincere wish to express my gratitude and admiration to Idries Shah
And the Sufi's whose many works over the years have led to my greater
Understanding of the truth of our existence here, and shown me the reality of
what the divine actually is.
I also wish to express undying gratitude to Octagon Press in London who continue
to disseminate his wisdom, and whose permission I greatly appreciate in my efforts
to help others.

BALBOA.
PRESS
A DIVISION OF HAY HOUSE

Balboa Press books may be ordered through booksellers or by contacting:

Balboa Press
A Division of Hay House
1663 Liberty Drive
Bloomington, IN 47403
www.balboapress.com.au
1-(877) 407-4847

ISBN: 978-1-4525-0429-2 (sc)
ISBN: 978-1-4525-0430-8 (e)

Because of the dynamic nature of the Internet, any web addresses or links contained in
this book may have changed since publication and may no longer be valid. The views
expressed in this work are solely those of the author and do not necessarily reflect the
views of the publisher, and the publisher hereby disclaims any responsibility for them.

Ramtha quote copyright © 1999, 2004 JZ Knight. Used with permission.

The author of this book does not dispense medical advice or prescribe the use
of any technique as a form of treatment for physical, emotional, or medical
problems without the advice of a physician, either directly or indirectly. The
intent of the author is only to offer information of a general nature to help you
in your quest for emotional and spiritual well-being. In the event you use any
of the information in this book for yourself, which is your constitutional right,
the author and the publisher assume no responsibility for your actions.

Any people depicted in stock imagery provided by Thinkstock are models,
and such images are being used for illustrative purposes only.
Certain stock imagery © Thinkstock.

Printed in the United States of America

Balboa Press rev. date: 03/14/2012

Dedication

I dedicate these words to my Taryn Joy, my Rose of Baghdad

Who made me whole.

And to the only other two stars that shine in my night sky, Dane and Leah.

Who was also, as well as being a vegetarian, known to have been aware of 'The mind of God', which led to his belief that there was one single power binding everything together, which later led to the statement that – 'Metaphysics is the only true Science'.

One day — whether in this life or in those that follow — when the marketplace no longer offers you any more, there will be a great emptiness, a great pull, and a great desire to become all. Then you too will look forward to every moment on the plateau, for there the wind is like strong fingers in your hair. Birds are taking flight to far-off nesting places, and the sun is brilliant with golden rods across your heavens. And when you do as I did and become — for that is the most important thing to you — I will welcome you where the Ram went, for the door to freedom, called knowledge, is there for you who will open your thought processes to a grander understanding and then live that understanding not outside of you but inside of you. When you have lived it, then you are finished here; then you are off to a new adventure. And the adventures that lie beyond this place are grander and more spectacular than you can imagine. So pliable are you in light that you can travel to outer space or to inner space, wherever you desire to go.

The Master Ramtha
The White Book

PREFACE

DURING MY TIME ON THE EARTH there are certain observations I have made that I feel cannot be overlooked.

Some people may even benefit from them and this is why I am writing my story. The true nature of our existence here has never been fully understood by a greater portion of the population. I give thanks to the forces that have led me to a position of greater understanding and which have enabled me to stand back from the day-to-day workings of the earth and truly observe what is happening around me.

My understanding comes from the ability to remain: 'In the Moment.'

As Eckhart Tolle attests, time and again in his books, this ability is truly a gift but it is a gift we give ourselves through commitment and practice. It will open one's eyes to the extent that the human race has succumbed to our mechanical and often automated existence.

We have in fact, lost the ability to view our lives with any sense of clarity. If we were able to, we would mourn all that we have lost. I have seen that life on earth is no more than a process of learning for the soul; of evolution. Nothing more.

Most are not even aware that we have a soul, let alone what it is for, or even where it is within us. Some of our habits we might find more interesting than others but a habit is none the less a habit and will, without interference, continue to dull our senses to the point where we are no longer in contact with the purpose of our existence.

Our existence is mostly mechanical in nature; our very thoughts become automated and repetitive. As any of the Spiritual Masters that have ever been on the earth will tell you, our greatest handicap to achieving a state of perfection in any form, is the incessant internal dialogue we conduct within what we assume is our mind. Our reactions to events in the world around us are also mechanical and repetitive. They are automatic reactions not considered responses.

It goes without saying that any of the more subtle feelings that arise from our consciousness have also become machine-like and habitual. And the worst of it is that most people will deny having any habits in the first place.

It could be said that we have entered a situation where we no longer have the ability to listen to our heart, the only one of our organs that can connect us to God, our soul and all that is real. People now spend most of their time in their heads, thinking about things. This is a gigantic trap because it allows the ego to have greater control and the ego will constantly and tirelessly remind us of our fears. It will remind us of mistakes we have made in the past and it will project past fears onto any future event. It never tires of this game.

If any evolution is to occur in a human being it will only achieve success after what is referred to as 'the death of the ego', has been achieved. This involves being able to create something of a permanent centre within us which is not subject to the dictates of thought.

The process or act of 'being in the moment' takes our attention away from the brain and this is a positive step to be sure. It quietens the ego so that after some practice some sort of evolution may occur within.

The only purpose of the earth, and indeed any inhabited planet is solely for the evolution of the soul. I offer my story as an example of that and draw upon observations gleaned from the Sufi's and other sources. This includes my own initiation with a spiritual Master.

The things that I have learned have been an invaluable guide for my process of awakening and healing; we are only here to find our way to our real home. It is my firm belief that there are no people on the earth who do not have some type of problem or early conditioning to overcome and those that appear to be deliriously happy are really just better actors than the rest of us.

The approach of 2012 has been much heralded in various forms, not all of them positive in nature. 2012 is the beginning of what may be called a 'Golden Age.' These events occur only every 26,000 years on earth and can be likened to a period of much higher spiritual consciousness. We need this higher consciousness badly.

When I look around I see a world where human beings are so conditioned to the pace of their lives that survival becomes a matter of mechanics where people have no knowledge of what is real; of the heart that beats within us. There seems little time for their fellow human beings.

There was a time in ancient Egypt where God consciousness and spiritual practice were the norm and elevated states of awareness and consciousness reigned supreme; this time is about to befall us again. Egyptologists, fossicking around the pyramids and hieroglyphics, view only the most superficial remains of what once was. There was yet another Egypt, long before what now remains where real knowledge of the true state of the universe and God existed.

In this more ancient Egypt there were schools; schools of mystery that produced what may be called mystics; people who understood and practised all the physical laws that the universe had to offer and that could produce what many may have called miracles. It would seem incredulous to many people that in this pre-history Egypt there also existed certain schools which were a lesser version of the mystery schools except that these were to eventually become a model for the basis of Christianity; albeit thousands of years before Christ was born.

They used public repetition of various prayers, hymns, and responses at the appropriate junctures. There were special holidays to be observed, and many symbols integrated within them. History though, as is the tendency with human beings, has long since forgotten their original meanings. That which still exists today remains a hollow remainder of the original truths it once held.

A student was spending time with a sage.

'If anyone were to say; 'Stand on your head and you will attain eternal felicity,' some people would do it,' said the student. 'People thirst for directions, however inept.'

'My child,' answered the sage; 'That is precisely what most of them have been doing these past ten thousand years.'

CONTENTS

Chapter One

'WHY AM I DIFFERENT?'

believe that at some point the Pope publicly admitted that the devil did not in fact exist. On this we are in agreement. There is no need for the devil because hell is right here where we are; the earth.

I suppose I must be honest here and admit that at this point, the day I'm writing this, I am fully aware that our souls, being only interested in their own evolution, carefully examine the upcoming life they are about to enter; the parents are chosen beforehand, the star sign, and in fact everything that will cause an emotional response in the body during that life is considered.

Even your body is chosen for a reason, and your soul guides will not let you begin your next life unless you can emotionally deal with all that will befall you. There are no doubt various arguments as to whether or not suicide is factored in or if this is a decision people make with their own free will and therefore cuts short the life they are meant to live.

This is not an escape. From what I can see there is a chance they may have something of an uncomfortable 'crossing over' and will be made to relive the circumstances that drove them to that point in the first place, in a later incarnation. Reincarnation is a fact; one that is hidden from us.

Whatever the truths about such things, the reality is that we are here in this world to live our lives to the best of our ability. We will take into the next world every memory we have.

My earliest memory is from kindergarten. I vividly recall that I used to keep my right hand hidden under the desk while I was playing with blocks because I had a deformed right hand.

Apparently the umbilical cord had been wrapped around the fingers while I was in the womb and they did not form correctly. I was later told that I had surgery, entailing 150 stitches which made the hand usable. I had no memories of that experience but I did have an overwhelming sense of being different and feeling inadequate.

I was always uncomfortable about letting people see my hand and this feeling would remain with me for at least forty-five years or so. In addition, I discovered later, that my birth had been difficult and it had impacted dramatically on the opportunity for me to bond with my mother.

Only those who have experienced the same sort of thing can understand the effect this can have. In my case I know it led me to build a wall around my heart; a wall so high and so impenetrable that no one can ever hurt me. At least that is what I wanted. It took quite some time before I found out what had happened on that day; or what had failed to happen.

I have since learned that my mother's personality was that of a perfectionist and she wanted to present my father with a boy for his firstborn. I am now suspecting, with my knowledge of human nature, that she felt hurt or perhaps even ashamed that she had created an imperfect child. As it was, she did not hold me in her arms until the third day of my life.

Unfortunately, by then it was too late. I suspect my impenetrable wall was well and truly in place and would remain there for at least fifty years. So it was obvious that my soul had elected to engage more than one handicap for this, my latest visit to earth.

In fact, through most of my schooling I suffered from the same feelings of imperfection and denial of what I was. I apparently was liked by some people, but when someone I didn't know got word of my deformity I was extremely reluctant to show them the hand and made up some excuse about how it had occurred (since I didn't really know what the truth was). It is also worthy of note that my parents never ever talked about the hand or how it affected me; a symptom of their own denial as well, I would think.

So, my feelings about myself persisted all through to the sixth grade without change. My plan for coping was to keep a low profile and not attract too much attention from either teachers or students with whom I was not familiar. Most of the time it worked, save for the occasional question from an inquisitive older student, which always tended to embarrass me – but, I survived it.

The next most significant event in my life was the day I started high school. This was a terrifying day for me; a new school, new people, new teachers, but significantly not a new me. It was a whole new group of people that would ask to see my hand; again my only friend was my right hand pocket, a haven against all the prying eyes.

I viewed the world as a frightening place. I didn't know who I was, I didn't feel comfortable around new people (this was to be a life-long problem) and high school was a scary place. But I eventually found my place and even some people that I would call friends. Having found a few people that were able to befriend me, I settled back into what you could vaguely call a routine, one that I could live with. I knew when to hide my hand, and I knew what to say when someone new asked how it became like that. Life, I thought, was relatively tolerable.

As time went on though, some of the boys that were part of the 'in' group found me sort of amusing at times. There was a tendency by one of them 'Norman' Ray, to impose on me physically when he felt the need for me to amuse others (I was only average in stature at that point), but all in all I quite liked him and it probably made me feel of some value on some deeper level, which I needed.

It was at this time, the advent of black and white television, that a program called 'The Samurai' began to appear. This was to be of significance for me. There were two things that I had perceived about the program of which I had been previously unaware. The first of these was an awareness of the Samurai ethic; that there was a code by which they lived. They believed it was possible for a human being to possess greater than average skills, if one had first mastered the fear of death. In other words you could enjoy everything that life had to offer, but you walk with the knowledge that death is your shadow. The second most intriguing feature for me was that the program depicted a ninja, who, after entering a deep state of meditation, became totally invisible to his passing enemies.

You will understand why this appealed to me.

I have since discovered that this is entirely within the bounds of credibility. At thirteen or fourteen years of age I wondered why these events had some significance for me. I was later to learn that our souls will remember all of our past lives whilst in the womb but as soon as we take our first breath at birth the veils of forgetfulness descend and it is all forgotten. But what is not forgotten is the soul's only task; which is to find its way home. These two events within 'The Samurai' were to prove highly relevant in my life.

Furthermore, about that time in my life, I suppose in a way you could say that I was fortunate in as much as, being born a Catholic, I was subjected to the usual prerequisite first communion, confessions and confirmations etc.. According to my mother all these ceremonies had to be enacted in order to keep me out of hell.

But during the indoctrination process, usually carried out by nuns, I was aware enough even at that age to notice the absence of a degree of sincerity in these people. I'm sure that on a deeper level, they believed what they were saying, but I was aware that their own hearts were conspicuously absent. They repeated all by rote; this was a significant observation for me.

What then, was the truth? And where would 'I' find it? These things concerned me for quite a number of years; for most of my life in fact. It goes without saying that in most of organized religions, if you are aware enough, you can notice a degree of 'manufacture' in the clergy's assurances that we are 'sinners' even to the point of conspicuously raising their voices at the appropriate intervals.

The message is that we will eventually pay a price for our less than adequate humanity. I was later to discover, through the spiritual Masters, that much within organised religion has been omitted. This began long ago in a bid to control the populace. If anybody needs more proof of the fact that many, probably most, in organized religion are no more than mere mortals, and just as fallible as us, all you have to do is examine the number of crimes committed against children, particularly young boys. In fact, a distant member of my own family whom I only met once, many years later, who had been a member of the Christian Brothers was declared guilty of these very crimes whilst in charge of a boy's home in Western Australia. (It is my considered opinion that these people had no idea whatever of the truth of which Jesus or any of the other Masters spoke).

So there I was, a high school student, a Catholic, whatever that meant; a less than adequate human being in my own view and with a tendency to withdraw into myself if any physically threatening situation arose. I had no confidence in myself and I actually had no access whatsoever to emotions of any sort. I could laugh and occasionally I could make others laugh, but the only emotion I ever seemed to recognise or had access to was fear. It was not much of a life really, but it was all I had, so you learn to live with it.

There was one boy 'Morrison' was his name, and for some reason he instantly disliked me. That situation never changed. There were constant threats from him. I never actually knew why so I tended to stay out of his way as much as possible. Later I came to realise that this type of resentment in someone stems from past life issues; from another time and place. I had hurt him or he had hurt me – our souls remember the vibrations from past-life encounters.

The high school years flew by, my grades were never all that impressive, I was average, nothing more, nothing less. Unfortunately though I had a friend called Mark and we got on extremely well. The result was that we both had to repeat fourth form due to our distraction with each other. But what did begin to eventually worry me was the fact that some of the boys knew exactly what they wanted to do with their lives. Even in fourth form Mark knew he wanted to become a commercial artist. I had no idea what I was on earth for, or what I wanted to do next. I do recall that the career advisor called me to his office one day and asked me to choose a trade to look at when I had finished the year. I resented this. I didn't know who I was let alone what work I was to do on the planet. So ultimately, I was one big question mark.

What was wrong with me? Why wasn't I like everyone else? What the hell was my place here? So far, life was confusing enough without the advent of girls, but invariably they eventually appeared and of course, this served to further remind me of my deficiencies.

Mostly all I ever heard from others was that I was 'shy' and most were aware that I kept my hand hidden most of the time. That was to continue until probably my late thirties unfortunately. Eventually though I did meet, Susan Anne and we would end up getting married but I didn't know that through the nightmare that was adolescence.

After I left high school, I was entirely without direction. My friend Mark went to T.A.F.E. to begin his art course and I, after some time attempted to enrol in the same course because I also had some creative ability. However, this was not particularly successful. I suspect this was only because I didn't know what else to do and I wanted some companionship. In the end, I did absolutely nothing for a year and a half. Many years later my soul guides led me to a book that explained precisely why I didn't know what I wanted on earth but I will speak more of this later.

After one and a half years, my parents started making 'suggestions' about the possibility of me eventually finding some work. After repetitive conversations I was informed that I had an uncle who managed an insurance outlet and he could get me a job of some description. Eventually I began to see the strength of their argument; with an added bit of persuasion from Susan Anne who had entered my life by that time.

This I achieved and I suppose it was interesting to be earning money for a change but I was still within my own little world, and my perceptions were, after more than a year, telling me to look around myself at the people that worked in this city. Slowly but surely, some inner truths became obvious to

me. People walked around every lunch break with
dull expressions on their faces; no one was happy.
It was then I began to see the mechanical nature of
their lives. Probably some thought of themselves as
having good jobs and were really getting somewhere
but at nineteen I was already aware of an apparent
emptiness in life.

Eventually I couldn't stand it anymore and left
the company. That however put me right back where
I started. I still didn't know what I was here for, or
what I wanted. Not too long after, due to pressure
from parents and again from Susan Anne I relented
and returned to insurance, mostly to shut everyone
up. It is again worthy of note that ,at that age, my
thoughts regarding the attraction of the mysterious
east, namely the martial arts, took hold of me and
I joined a Karate club in north Sydney. Although I
now know that I was shamelessly over compensating
for my perceived inner deficiencies. But it made me
happy for quite some time to know that I seemed
to have lost my inner fear of danger on the streets
of any city.

Now at about twenty years of age and having
had a girlfriend for a couple of years or so, talk

started to revolve around the word marriage. This talk unfortunately coincided with my decision to again leave the insurance company. I just could not stand the mechanical existence any longer; it just became unbearable. So in the end although I did not particularly want to marry, (mind you I had no real complaints about Susan) I just didn't know what the hell I wanted, but with my inherent state of disconnection from any real emotion or direction or access to a heart or even a knowledge of my life's purpose I heard myself saying 'Get married, yeah I suppose so... why not?'

So, at twenty-one years of age and me without a job, we got married and remained so for twenty-five years.

At this point, I'd like to pause again and explain more about the whole process of life on earth as I have come to understand it.

In other dimensions (heaven) we are complete unto ourselves – we have both male and female energy inherent within us and we want for nothing. But, as we prepare to enter the earth for yet another turn on the merry-go-round we are faced with choices: does our soul need to be male or female for this life and what will give our soul the experience that it needs for this 'lesson.'

Hence we choose and upon reaching puberty we feel urged to find our missing counterpart energy. We do not feel complete without a partner; unless of course loneliness is a necessary ingredient that the soul requires at that point in its evolution. So we marry.

At least this is how I am able to make sense of it all. There are some souls that may become confused about gender at this point and I put that down to past life habits. Or perhaps that confusion is also something they have chosen to be a lesson in this life.

For a time I remained unemployed, while Susan worked. I was still lost, but I amused myself with my martial arts training for as much as two hours a day at times, until I eventually had to return to work. I found a job as a cleaner for a time, but even this didn't enable me to find myself; whoever that might have been. If you think I sound confused it is because I was!

I had a friend Roger who shared my interest in photography and this triggered thoughts in me of making films for a living. I left the cleaning job and tried to get a job near the Australian Broadcasting Commission

The closest I could get was a job in a film laboratory next door to them. I stayed there for about six years or so. During this time my first daughter was born. She arrived on November 16, 1975 at ten past four in the afternoon. That was the most significant day of my life and remains so to this day.

However, as a young father I was a total failure. Susan, although unsure of herself and doubting her abilities as a mother, somehow got through it all. I on the other hand had trouble connecting with anyone in the real world, let alone a brand new life. I didn't even understand what love was let alone how to give it to another so I stood in the back ground.

After a while though, the bond to Taryn Joy would become the most powerful thing I had ever experienced in my life; that I ever *would* experience in this life.

I eventually did get a job at the ABC in the staging and props area. A class three licence was a necessity. I kept going with my martial training

however and experimented with different types of
practice but I never truly felt I was 'at home'.

My second daughter Leah was born on the 30th
of September, 1978 and again I was pleased at the
feelings that fatherhood produced in me. But as far
as my life was concerned, I was still confused. I tried
many times to leave the area that I was employed
in by applying for various internal courses that were
available within the ABC; floor manager, producer,
director ... but I failed to gain entry to any of
them.

Despite the fact that I had gained a greater sense
of my own creative abilities, as far as the ABC was
concerned I was still not up to the mark.

I admit, that after a time, this made me a little
embittered. My skills in my martial arts training did
help me to overcome the feelings of unworthiness.
At that point I was qualified to teach.

But in the main, I really did not appreciate what
I had and what and who I was, but this is where
the universe, or more correctly, my own soul guides
began the manipulation that was their 'soul' purpose
to lead me to greater understanding of myself and
the life I was meant to live.

Looking back from this point in time I can see that our lives are directed, if not manipulated so we experience what we need to experience so we can learn what we need to learn.

I came into contact with a man who was to become a good friend; Adam Bindoff from Tasmania. At that time I was twenty-eight years old. Adam was a man of great wit and possessed a wry sense of humour that quickly grew on me. He also spoke in an unhurried, considered manner; he was never really in a hurry to do or say anything. As time passed I discovered a reason for this; Adam was also a man of intellect and like me, some time ago he had developed an interest in the true nature of things and his spiritual Self. His own search had led him into spiritual bookshops some years earlier and also like me, he had a desire to find out more about all that was lacking in organized religion. He saw the inherent emptiness in the world just as I did.

People are placed in our lives at very specific times for very specific reasons; there are no accidents, and there are no coincidences.

Adam's own search had led him to an area of investigation that was precisely where I needed to get to (according to my guides). The reason for Adam's unhurried speech and precise answers was that for some time he had been following a line of thinking that led him to the Sufi's and Sufic thought.

Through this he had cultivated the ability to remain 'In the Moment.' This may seem like an extremely obscure term when first heard but it is a crucially important one. This is because humans tend to spend much of their time in their heads, using their brains, held captive by their thoughts and this is not the way to inner peace. We rarely ever cease the continual internal dialogue within our heads, much of it with our tongues in continual motion.

Many spiritual teachings hold the 'ego' responsible for this. The ego likes to continually replay events from our past; it spends a lot of time in the past. Our emotions on the other hand seem to like living in the future. So with our thoughts in the past and our emotions focussed on the future we spend little or no time in the Now!

Apart from the ego there are several control centres within our bodies which are called Chakras. These correspond to the glands of the endocrine system; any one of which can be in control at any one time. The replaying of past events tends to recreate exactly the same emotions that we originally felt when we experienced those past events.

It is easy to see how this particular habit is a misuse of our energy and emotions. It is not until you are able to stay 'in the moment' that you become aware of every single thing that is happening around you; *And within you.*

If any evolution is to occur as a human being then staying in the moment is a necessity for us.

With every single thought streams of energy fly off from your own aura and into the universe. Depending on the thoughts, not only does it have an impact beyond our own selves but it can be a major cause of weariness in our bodies. The brain/ego, if not mastered, can be like a naughty, demanding child of about two to three years of age and unfortunately, for those who do not practise and learn self-mastery this remains so for the rest of their lives.

So, what does one do with a demanding child responding from instinct and lacking in mature self-discipline? That is the question Jesus, the Sufi's and just about every single spiritual Master that has ever come to this earth has given the same answer:

you respond with compassion and you embrace the child but you give it something to do which will enable it to learn and to practise, self mastery. This also gives it something to do; something to occupy itself productively as opposed to the constant usually negative reaction which is produced by the immature and undisciplined ego.

This is the part of our consciousness which causes most if not all of our problems. It also impedes our ability to evolve and is responsible for all the useless thoughts; the fear of the future and the worrying imaginings which rarely become reality and the continual reminders of when we made mistakes in the past.

This constant process of the internal dialogue is what leads us to mechanical reactions instead of considered responses. This is a state where our behaviour becomes habitual. We find ourselves in a quagmire from which it is impossible to escape without the greatest effort.

The Eastern response to this quandary has been to teach and practice mindfulness. There are many practices which enable us to become more centred, balanced and mindful of our thoughts, our feelings and our actions. The goal is to become a silent observer where we are aware of our thoughts and feelings as they occur, but we do not act on them. In this way the over active 'Brain' or 'Ego' is placed where they can do little or no harm.

This is not something, which can be achieved overnight but once practice has begun, it will eventually lead to our escape from the Ego's enslavement of us. One form of practice is to become aware of the energy centres, or Chakras of the body. When we choose to focus on one of the chakras it can help us to remain centred throughout the day. To fully understand the chakra system it is helpful to study what each chakra represents and does. You can access this information online or buy a book.

Such practices of mindfulness will put us on a path which takes us to all greater truths and ultimate enlightenment. Through such practices we can still the over-active mind; discipline the demands of the ego and occupy the 'naughty child.' In truth this 'child' is not 'naughty' but merely immature. It is like any 'child' who has not learned 'Mastery of Self' and thus has no choice but to react instinctively and often unthinkingly. Just as a real child learns best through a compassionate, loving approach, so does our 'inner child.'

When we have calmed the turmoil within our minds; stilled the restless, demanding ego and found a place of balance we will be in a position where our 'guides' may appear to help us further on the path. At this point we may also discover why we are here in the first place.

It was as I came closer to this time that my son Dane Francis was born. It was the first of December 1981. After two girls I admit that I was hoping to have a boy. It was a day of great joy. But life had more challenges in store for both me and my wife.

I have wondered since if it was because I placed a great deal of pressure on Susan Anne to have another child, to produce a boy, although I was unaware at the time that I was putting her under pressure. Perhaps she was also pressuring herself. Whatever the reason, not long after Dane's birth, Susan developed a tumour around the saliva gland.

While traumatic for her this was also upsetting for me. It was at this point that that I came to understand that I had a fear of cancer and this created much greater stress within me as we went through the operation to remove the tumour and continual post operative checks.

But like so many experiences in my life, this one also pushed me toward greater and deeper understandings. Later I came to believe that people tend to form lumps within themselves as a result of a negative self image. My wife later told me that she so badly did not want to disappoint me with another girl that she felt extremely stressed. I am sure that stress contributed to the growth of the tumour. *All our thoughts and feelings and emotions create; there are no exceptions. The speed at which they create is governed only by your own spiritual level.*

As all is decreed in other dimensions, my time with Adam slowly came to a close. He returned to Tasmania. By then I suppose you could say that I had been awakened to the possibility of the existence of a greater truth.

Although still very interested in Sufi thinking and reading their truths, it was obvious that I had no future within the ABC so when a job came up at TCN 9 I took the opportunity and left. Unfortunately, the job only lasted one year. This was the year that the presenter, Ray Martin, began his lunchtime show.

As is common with commercial television, as viewer
habits change so do employment opportunities and
so I was left without a job again.

At that time I had, in an effort to increase my skills,
undertaken a course in film production techniques at
TAFE (Technical and Further Education) College. It
was a four-year course and I did learn a lot there, but
with a family to support, I had to get a job quickly.
I called my brother Frank a handyman/ rubbish
remover and asked if he needed an employee at that
point. His answer was yes and so I was employed
once more. I also had a part time job at Harold
Park as a camera operator on the nights the trotting
meetings were run.

At this point in time I was twenty-nine years
old and I began to feel my old discontentment
returning, I was grateful to have a job but it was
manual work and I still had a vague feeling that
I was here for some other purpose; the uneasiness
continued to grow in me. I was very happy with
my children and I loved them dearly. After being
married for some time I was vaguely aware that
Susan Anne was somehow making all the decisions
regarding the family but I was still unaware of

who or what I was so I made no effort to change anything at home.

I was attracted to many of the pieces of spiritual literature that were found in the bookshops at that time and I continued to search for more answers, although the Sufi's were never far from my thoughts – let's face it, the truth is the truth.

> *There is no inconsequential man. But what he has done to himself, and what has been done to him – can make him inconsequential.*
>
> From a collection by Idries Shah

My brother has a good heart, he would help anyone who needed it, but after a year or so at my job I became severely disheartened and began to feel a failure yet again:

'Who the hell was I? 'Why the hell am I here?'

I loved my children, I thought I loved my wife but I was not happy. Why wasn't I happy? What the hell was happiness anyway? But in the end it always came back to: 'Why am I here?'

As I was later to discover, negative energy just attracts more negative energy. I arrived at a point where I could not stand my job anymore. I can recall thinking to myself while loading rubbish onto the back of my brother's truck: 'I wish I could have an accident so that I didn't have to do this job anymore.'

Well within fifteen minutes I had subliminally created just that outcome. While throwing an empty oil container on the back of the truck one of the small fingers on my deformed right hand got caught in the handle; I had broken it. My thought assured that my inner wishes would be realised. What a powerful mind we have within us…

I got my wish. I was officially on compensation and not working until my finger healed. Unfortunately it did not. I waited for about nine months, even to the extent of having pins inserted to assist the process.

During this time I went for many long walks and all the time pondering what my future held, if anything. However, my inner feelings of self loathing and lack of direction persisted on a daily basis: I hated myself. And I hated life and I certainly did not want to remain. I was perpetually surrounded with my own negative energy. I can't recall if I took any of that out on my family; I certainly hope I did not. But as my finger apparently did not want to heal and finally I was persuaded to have the tip of it removed at the break. Following that little operation I now had to decide what lay in store for the rest of my life.

Clearly I did not want to go back to manual work, so fortuitously, George, a friend from Harold Park told me about a job going at a video duplication firm Video 8. I applied and was accepted.

Chapter Two

AS YOU SOW,
SO SHALL YE REAP?

After immersing myself in decidedly negative feelings about my job with my brother, the type of work it was, and my lack of any inner knowing about what lay in store for me next, added to my perpetual self loathing, it was the following couple of months which turned out to be the start of a significant change in my awareness.

I still kept reading about the Sufis and also other books which came my way including 'The Celestine Prophecy' by James Redfield and I thank him for his quite significant work. But regardless of all this, after beginning a new job and starting to think that my life might make some sort of sense again, I noticed some subtle changes within my body, so I made an appointment with my doctor.

As is the way of things, a couple of tests were necessary and then my doctor referred me to some sort of specialist – apparently it was some type of lump within me, and as I left her surgery that day I will never forget her parting words – after having her own mother die of cancer, she told me I was 'going to visit hell' for three months ... she was right.

However, now that I know the power of words I would question whether or not she was right to say it.

I remember sitting in the specialist's office the day he told me the full story. My body was pumping out hormones that are normally only found in women and this was a sure sign that there was a problem somewhere within my body.

This news put me in shock, quite literally. Fortunately he had an examination table in his office and I needed to lay on it; if I hadn't I would have passed out. I suspect at that point my wife was already aware of the full extent of this news, but this was the first time I had heard the full story.

I was not aware of it at that point but even though I was told that that particular type of cancer is curable, you just don't believe them; I felt I was looking at death. My first words to my wife when we got back to the car were: 'But I haven't achieved anything yet' (Mind you I didn't know what it was that I wanted to achieve.)

So began the medical profession's cancer merry-go-round.

It was a very difficult three months. There was one visit to hospital every month for a barrage of chemical cocktails, one of which, for some reason, makes you dry retch every hour on the hour all through the night. Then, following the two day visit, you are to return home but since you are literally being poisoned you are unable to consume very much food or sustenance.

That part of the procedure lasts for one week and then, the following week you begin to feel 'almost' passable. My wife although fearful, did the best she could during the process and since I had only just started a new job she managed to go into my work and help out so our income would not suffer. I can only thank my employers for their consideration at that time. After that process I still had, for some years, to go for regular blood tests etc. to keep a check on it. The fear of a reappearance however remained with me for at least five years.

There is absolutely no doubt in my mind that I was the one who had created the cancer within myself after my constant self-loathing and disgust at my lack of direction or significant success in life. There was also a component of involvement on the part of my mother but I will discuss that later.

There had been two small tumours on the surface of my right testicle, one six millimetres and also one three millimetres. Unfortunately it took them quite a time to find them. I can recall my first visit to the hospital prior to the operation. Since there had been some difficulty in locating the source of my problem, (it could have been anywhere in the endocrine system) a visiting expert from the United States was called in to refer on the case. Apparently I was an anomaly. On that first day I was visited by nurses and trainee doctors from everywhere in the hospital all day but toward the end of the day, the doctor from the U.S. appeared at my bed with a gaggle of several nurses and doctors and asked me if he could 'feel' the area in question and check for any signs.

Now at that point, I was sure that he was a very nice man and an excellent surgeon but to have to stand there in front of the nurses and lift my gown while he felt my balls was a little on the embarrassing side. Fortunately there was one nurse there who understood my plight and tastefully hid her smirk while the ordeal proceeded. All in all my next memory was after the operation. I awoke to see Susan Anne holding my bed sheet high to peer underneath to check on the outcome. I don't blame her since it would affect her sex life for some time to come had both been removed. (There had always been some doubt as to whether both had been affected.)

But as is the nature of men, upon waking, there are usually more than apparent signs that all is well. Apparently she was quite happy and I was more than a little pleased to experience that familiar erect feeling again. Susan was never a person to beat around the bush.

If one chooses to surround oneself with less than happy thoughts, as I said the energy must affect something in the material realm. My negativity was directed inwards, so the two areas that were affected were the solar plexus chakra and the abdominal chakra.

The purpose of the solar plexus centre is to ensure a balance between the spiritual life and the earthly life. I had a second tumour behind my pancreas, which was behind the solar plexus; I definitely was not in balance with life and did not have a trust in the natural flow of the universe. The lower abdominal centre (reproductive organs etc.) when out of balance, demonstrates an inability to express feelings adequately and a suppression of natural needs, which was a perfect match with what I was feeling in the previous year. In the end, I was told that at the rate that the hormone level was increasing I would have been dead in twelve weeks.

Apparently I did have a purpose in life I just didn't know what it was yet and I can only surmise that my guides and angels were very good at their jobs. I can only say, thank you all.

I would ask you to note that: 'As you sow so shall you reap' should be taken in the most literal sense. In essence, as you think so you create. Whatever energy you transmit or emit will come straight back to you without fail. It is a lack of awareness which prevents people from recognising this fact.

Together with the fact that since most people do not live according to Christ's, or any other person's precepts (even if they fully understood what they were) life travels on regardless of what is stated within organized religion. We can see so much more of the world once we separate ourselves from the mechanics of the 'survival' mode that appears so predominant.

There are so many situations where it becomes clear that people have very little control over themselves, and it is never more obvious then when people drive their cars. Suddenly changing lanes in front of you without warning as they remember something or somewhere that they have forgotten to be or do. And they are oblivious to the fact that when they pull out of a side street in front of you, causing you anger, long after they have forgotten the incident, karma dictates that someone else is going to do the same thing to them. No one escapes karma, instant or otherwise as was duly noted by John Lennon.

There are times however, where it is difficult to observe the results of our actions. This can be attributed to the difference in spiritual levels which people have attained. But have no doubt, your energy will always return to you without fail. In a person of otherwise good intentions it may take quite some time for enough negative energy to build up around them before it will affect or effect something in the material world. People do not appear to be aware that after having a bad day, a day of negative thoughts and emotions the end result ... let's say reversing their car into a small post ... may not occur for two months or so.

Another karmic teaching which makes sense to me is that if you should kill a person, then in your next life karma returns the favour and that soul will then return into your life and kill you. This is not clearly understood and yet it offers a perfect explanation for those who appear to lead exemplary lives and yet are killed with no apparent motive. All our actions incur a debt.

Now at this point I have to note that my father never drank alcohol and I see it as a conscious decision on the part of my soul before entering my body to choose him as a father, since alcohol is not conducive to spiritual growth. The parents and every facet of the coming life are considered before the soul enters the earth. Alcohol, in my opinion, can only be thought of as a handicap so I now readily accept that clearly most of my life had been pre-arranged to be full of handicaps.

But when all had settled down after the cancer threat, I returned to my job, and after some months I decided that a celebration was in order. Due to pressure from my friends in my twenties, although I didn't like the taste of it, I learned to like the feeling of release that alcohol gave me so I got very drunk one night. Susan was unimpressed, quite understandably, but it was something I needed to do at that point. Alcohol played a bigger part in my life after that.

So even with the apparent cloud of the return of the cancer, life I suppose became tolerable for a while. The game played on. I had a job and I kept on reading whatever my intuition (or guides) led me to. Many of what we think are our own thoughts are placed in our consciousness by our guides and I know that much of what I have learned has come from material or books which have been brought to me.

But after one or two years it became obvious to me that there was little opportunity to really achieve anything or gain a higher position in the company for which I worked. After reading James Redfield I had the good fortune (or good guidance) to come across a book called 'Conversations with God' by Neale Donald Walsh. This book made me think that there was a light at the end of a very long, dark tunnel. The book confirmed much of my own thoughts about the truth of our reality (the Earth and God) but my own discontent returned as it always did. And with it came my old friend – self loathing. And the bouts of alcohol indulgence persisted.

I could not see anywhere else to go at my job. I didn't understand it at the time but I began to look for another job in what I thought was an inconspicuous manner. Apparently it was not all that inconspicuous. I began writing letters to obtain interviews from other employers but someone going through my garbage bin came across them and I was again left without a job. So at thirty- three years of age what the hell was I going to do next?

This highlights what human beings may refer to as self-sabotage. It is an extremely common occurrence, both in work related issues and relationships. My subconscious was really on the ball. What I really wanted had been created. *All our thoughts, emotions and feelings create.*

This concept is perhaps more clearly understood by considering that our souls have a much higher vibratory rate than anything which exists in the material world.

If you toss a pebble into a small puddle after the rain, what then happens to the surface of the water? You will see the ripples travel from the centre of the puddle, right to the edge of the water and immediately return to the centre. Exactly the same thing occurs with everything we think, feel and do. They all carry either a positive or negative charge. And please note that the universe is an identical reflection of the surface of the puddle: 'As above so below' with the significant exception that 'thoughts' and anything else we emit travel faster than light, and come straight back to us. A low spiritual awareness can mean a couple of months delay in the time it takes to affect the matter around us and the more spiritually developed we become, the more powerful the effect of our thoughts.

By this time our old house at Terrey Hills had required various repairs, all of which I had attempted myself. It seems that I was quite successful by all reports. Susan Anne suggested that I possessed sufficient skills to become a handyman. I seriously considered this prospect and was encouraged by the fact that my father had built our own family home before I was born. It seems I had inherited his skills. It didn't dawn on me until later that this was yet another part of the plan that the divine had organised for me.

Around this time I went to Hornsby with Susan Anne to look for a new lounge suite. We did not find what we wanted but on the way out I walked past a newsagent and my eye was 'led' to a white book at the end of the shop. I walked to it immediately. My guides had just arranged the whole trip to get me to find 'Conversations With God Book Two' which I wanted and needed to read. In the end, I read all of the series of books by Neale Donald Walsh and I have many times thanked God for sending him to us. He is a man who was fortunate enough in one of his past lives to have done an amount of spiritual work which put him in touch with his higher self. The higher self may be regarded as a portion of our soul that largely remains in higher dimensions and which can act as a guide as required. This usually happens when the spiritual level in the earth body has risen high enough to make connection possible.

One particularly relevant piece of information I gleaned from Neale Donald Walsh and others was that we are given signs from the divine on a regular basis but this unfortunately remains largely ignored by the human race. This is more common in those who live in developed societies and there are relatively unaffected portions of the human race including native Americans and Aborigines who remain more in touch with such 'signs' or energies.

This ancient wisdom has always been with us but it has been subjected to denial, suppression or destruction by the major religions.

I was inspired by this knowledge to learn more. I wanted to better understand both the manner and extent of such signs. This can be done through books, crystals, angel cards or anything which will put you in touch with your intuition. These 'tools' access your inner wisdom by circumventing the 'ego' or 'rational' mind. What works for one may not work for another so I advise you to explore and experiment.

The book which came to me was Signposts, by Denise Linn a native American. It is largely a dictionary containing a comprehensive list of the signs that most of our soul guides in the divine call upon to point us in a certain direction. I use the book frequently because I feel that the signs are extremely important.

To my mind there is a little game that is played by the divine that says that we all have free will. This is a fallacy as far as I am concerned. It may appear that we choose to go left at the next corner or we may choose to turn right but the reality is that we are being guided. As far as your guides are concerned, all that matters is 'getting you to the situations that your soul sought to experience when it chose to be born into this world'.

At this point in my life I know beyond any doubt whatsoever that free will is an illusion: 'What has been written shall come to pass.' If you are meant to board a flight overseas on a certain day at a certain time, if that was not part of that which your soul elected to experience then something will happen that will stop you. You will miss the train, the flight will be cancelled, the airport will be snowed in, something, whatever it may be, will stop you getting on that plane.

Another part of this game revolves around the fact that your guides cannot, and will not, tell you what to do next, or how to do it, or when to do it. I have had huge problems in this life through not knowing what is the right thing to do next. Decisions were always difficult for me. Susan Anne on the other hand always knew what to do. So it was easy for me to allow her to make all the decisions regarding the family. Her attitude was always one of: 'Just get on with it.'

She had absolutely no interest in believing in God; her focus was purely on day-to-day life and paying the bills. From what I could see, for her everything was only black or white, no shades of grey whatsoever. She did not seem to be as sensitive to things in the way that I was forced to be but we all have our own paths to walk and we walk them in our own way. My way was very different.

My way was to be able to find myself and to be able to recognize the signs that the universe was sending me whilst on the right path. The only way that you are able to know if you are on track ... following your soul's purpose ... is by being aware enough to recognise the signs your guides send you.

I have since discovered that crows are quite a favourite with my guides. Many times after I arrived at a point where my awareness had grown I would notice that after a thought passed through my mind, my guides would confirm the truth of that thought by arranging for a crow to fly parallel to my vehicle as I drove along. Alternatively, if the thought was contrary to my soul's path (in their eyes) the crow would be flying in the opposite direction toward the rear of my vehicle. Learn what the language of the divine is and keep an open mind about how your guides will choose to communicate with you.

Chapter Three

AN INNER LIGHT

'Cross and Christians, end to end,
I examined. He was not on the cross. I went
to the Hindu temple, to the ancient pagoda.
In none of them was there any sign. To the
uplands of Herat I went, and to Kandahar.
I looked. He was not on the heights or in the
lowlands. Resolutely, I went to the summit
of the fabulous mountain of Kaf. There only
was the dwelling of the [legendary] Anqa
bird. I went to the Kaaba of Mecca. He was
not there. I asked about him from Avicenna
the philosopher. He was beyond the range of
Avicenna ... I looked into my own heart.
In that, his place, I saw him. He was in no
other place.'

From – The Way of the Sufi, (Jalaludin Rumi)

Glancing back, in reflection, I have to note the value of the time I invested in a 'Self remembering' exercise back at the ABC. It proved to be of much value in separating me from the mechanical. It teaches you to be able to recognise what motivates the people around you. My wife many times called upon this knowledge in order to define the people around her so perhaps, when I remember that, I can see she was learning in her own way.

The more you know yourself the more you know about humanity.

It is often said that 'It takes all types' but I must disagree. If that is so then 'where are they all'.

There are only two reasons why anything will happen, or has ever happened on earth; there is only Love or Fear. Ponder this, if you can for a moment. Mind you, you must first be aware enough to 'catch' the thoughts as they flitter through your brain in the first place.

I was continuing to learn, continuing to practice and my life, at that time, had some sort of purpose. I was also working as a handyman and enjoying my children as they grew up.

I have to say at this point that I was very fortunate in so far as they were and are terrific children and to this day I remain very proud of them. My time with cancer put a little strain on the family and Taryn Joy (Taz) became a little distant while I was having the chemotherapy treatments. At eleven years of age the constant throwing up quite upset her and probably the thought of losing me worried her as well.

It was also about this time that I discovered after many years of physical activity in my various martial arts practice that I had some knee problems. After a lengthy search I looked around for some type of activity that did not involve the more strenuous stretches that are involved in kicking and to be honest the problems with my right hand did not allow me a great deal of confidence in the strength of my punching ability. Although I was quite able to defend myself in all situations.

Eventually I came across a Japanese art called Aikido which seemed to be a most suitable and to my mind, graceful art. It is a martial art but it is a synthesis of this, philosophy and religious belief. It is also non-violent. In fact it has been said that it is much like dancing. There were no kicking movements at all and although there was always time to deliver a punch in any particular movement it was not obligatory. This I found quite refreshing and together with the fact that the body continually moves in circular fashion around an 'opponent', greatly appealing. It was and is a beautiful art to behold, and more importantly the object was not to defeat an opponent but to throw him to the mats until his motivation to fight has left him.

To this day I'm still not sure whether I took to the fighting arts as overcompensation for my deficient hand or whether there was a much deeper reasoning. Perhaps I sensed that I would have to be a 'warrior' but I did not realise that it would be as a spiritual warrior.

I had many times visited psychics, one of which said that in a previous life I had been beheaded. I could see myself as a fighter or a soldier of some sort in my past lives. I wondered if it was the source of my lifelong fear of death.

It was at this point in my life that my guides again played a part by bringing me together with yet another man that I was 'supposed' to meet. My friend Eino Laidsaar made his first appearance. He was to be a significant influence on me. At first I gravitated toward him because he knew much about

Aikido and he taught in some smaller classes where there was more time to learn at a more comfortable pace, but as time went on I was attracted to some of his other qualities, some not so apparent to the naked eye. There was just something about him that I couldn't readily define.

Much later I was to discover that when a person has spent considerable time in pursuit of the universal truth, the ultimate truth of existence, people would then be attracted to them.

This occurs on a subliminal level at first and is the result of a glimmering of the inner light that shines within them. They have no need to infringe upon you, they do not actively pursue you like some religious zealots that call door to door, they just have an inner light that draws you near.

My spiritual education occurred slowly, I would ask a question here and then another one after the first answer was absorbed by my brain and bit by bit I began to understand that my new friend knew much about the universe and the ultimate source of all things. At the time I had met him he had already been meditating for twenty years and many truths had been presented to him.

As time went on and I learned more about Aikido and Eino (A-no) was always insistent on me undergoing grading tests which did not really appeal to me. I was uncomfortable about putting myself on display and having many people see my deformed hand but thankfully contact with Eino eventually led me to overcome these feelings.

I began to understand that no matter who you were or what condition your body was in, there was not one person on the earth that did not have a soul, and thereby unlimited access to all the realms that God has created. You should draw much strength from this. No-one can keep you from the unlimited love that is the right of our 'birth' and your entire existence.

Those who do not believe in God or in any purpose to this life and the life to come may well find that when they pass over it is challenging.

In the next world thoughts become reality at a much faster rate; the vibration is so much greater. So be careful what you believe. Perhaps ensure that you have some beliefs in the first place and put some thought into what those beliefs will be.

During most of my life, just about all of it in fact I only knew one purpose, I knew there was something else 'out there' and I had to keep going until I found the whole truth of it. Looking back I think I owe my wife an apology it must have appeared as quite a selfish attitude, although I did believe that I loved her, the problems in the relationship came later. God is a tough act to follow. I don't blame her for the eventual separation.

I have later discovered that I have been on the earth since nearly the beginning of man's first appearance here, as are many others at this time, which explains the rise in separations and divorces as many are beginning to realise that there is something missing in their lives. If they are fortunate they will come to understand that it is their connection to God that has been lost. My own inner quest was overpowering and slowly but surely it took a toll on the marriage. All I knew was that I had to find the truth.

Susan Anne had confided at one point that she had a feeling that she had been abused as a child and this was yet another straw on the camel's back that was our marriage. Our sex life was limited due to some of her inhibitions. I understand that a burden like that, for a woman, can be deeply embedded in the subconscious and could probably only be fully eradicated through hypnosis and the like, if not a past life regression. At that time, with my limited knowledge of the greater picture of all things I admit that our sex life left me wanting and my eye did wander but due to my own little quest I never actually had an affair. Which, given my belief in karma is all for the best.

So up until this point my life had largely been one of a complete lack of fulfilment save for my children. We had good times and there was no doubt whatsoever that I dearly loved my children and always will. They are great human beings but as a whole my life on the earth left me with a feeling of: 'What the hell was the point of this?'

I couldn't figure why I came here in the first place. At this point it had been one huge disappointment for me. Bereft of any joy whatsoever, save for the great pleasure that my children gave me, it was obvious that very little of what I wanted for my life was ever going to occur.

But I kept on going. The learning continued and I was now aware that much of the universal truth is hidden thanks in the main, to various factions within organised religion. My only truth (and this I had been aware of from an early age) was that I had to transcend the physical plane. This I attribute to my soul's knowing and hence my attraction to firstly 'the samurai' and then later to the eastern fighting arts and their spiritual undertones.

I am reminded of a portion of P.D.Ouspensky's book...'In Search of the Miraculous:' at one point in the book a man expressed an interest in knowing what his future held for him and many times I asked myself the exact same question. Many times I felt the urge to visit psychics to ascertain exactly that but psychics will only be shown some information, not all of it and I was not likely to find the answer I wanted. They will only be shown information that your guides feel will not change you attitudes or thinking to the extent that you will alter your behaviour and not experience what your soul has come here for.

'Today is what it is, because yesterday was what that was, and if today is like yesterday, tomorrow will be like today. If you want your tomorrows to be altered in any way you must start by altering today, and this can only happen by remaining in the moment.'

But to do this man is hampered because no one is 'in the moment' long enough to clearly see with any clarity the forces that have acted on him today. By saying 'forces' I speak of an awareness of a man's own conditioning which is largely all in place before he is even ten years old and sometimes much earlier. It is put in place largely by parents and relatives. Ultimately I was approaching a time where I began to understand that only some type of meditation was going to provide some of the answers for me to escape the prison that I felt I was in.

While I was slowly learning, my children were growing up faster than I would have liked. My girls were no longer playing netball and my son Dane had begun to play baseball which I found quite enjoyable. And also around this time Susan Anne's mother Olive suffered a stroke. I was only vaguely aware at that time of my own deficiencies and lack of a connection to my heart. Susan of course played the dutiful daughter and helped as much as she could but within myself I could feel the uneasy stirrings that heralded both my reluctance to get too involved at that time and what was to later become a pronounced fear of death on my part. My children of course loved their grandparents dearly and they were to watch over them often. Olive or 'Nanny' when the girls were smaller had much patience for them and often helped them make cakes while Susan and I went out.

'Darcy' my father in law played the kindly old grandparent and although the stroke caused him much anxiety he was not one to ever let it show. He like his daughter just 'got on with it'. To this day I haven't forgiven myself for my reactions to Olive's pain during those times. I was distant and lacking the compassion that should have been in me but my truth and the lessons that were to highlight the whole truth were to come much later.

My reading continued, and my questions to Eino continued, the answers sometimes tailored to my ability to understand them, which was fair enough. But in the end, although I was much more aware of the world, there comes a point where you have to put your money where your mouth is; I had not reached that point yet. I was developing an ability to remember some of my dreams and there were definitely messages within them. Your guides know exactly what you are thinking and feeling and when the time is right for a new piece of information it will come to you, if they feel you will understand the answer.

My girls were finding themselves in the world, making new friends as they grew. Taz however, when it was time for high school did not appear to be all that academic and found the process quite a handful. At one point she was having trouble with a group of girls who kept picking on her. They caused her so much pain that she wanted to leave the school. Susan tolerated Taz's complaints about this group for quite some time but in the end she gave my daughter a choice; she could leave the school only if she first obtained a job. Taz did find one, quite quickly as I recall and left the school. Leah after also having trouble with the school (a Catholic high school) opted to leave and was transferred to a public high school. Leah was quite creative and loved the creative aspects of art and often made her own clothes. Taz began work in a women's clothing store as a sales assistant, which was to be one of many similar jobs.

During this period I continued to be a handyman and occasionally my search for the 'intangible' missing part of me continued; sometimes to the dismay of my wife. There was a period where I did not feel like working at all, so money, at times, would only trickle into our lives. Eventually my 'quest' led to the appearance of clinical depression.

Naturally the loss of money coming in was a fearful experience for Susan. She wanted me well, or at least functional as quickly as possible.

I understand that money has a place in the world, but it later became clearer to me that we were on different paths in this world. Hers had a more material bent and mine was hellbent on the spiritual. I had a burning desire within me that no one could ever quell. I am reminded of another quote that may explain:

> *You have a duty to perform. Do anything*
> *else, do any number of things, occupy your*
> *time fully, and yet, if you do not do this task,*
> *all your time will have been wasted.*
>
> Jalaludin Rumi

Or, also, about the truth of us and our journey home,

Take some substance from here to there –
You will make no profit if you go with an
empty hand.

Omar Khayyam

They refer of course to our soul's evolution. Charles Darwin was severely limited in his perceptions because the only evolution possible for a human being is spiritual; it is only our souls that can evolve.

Evolution can be thought of as an expansion in a man, of those abilities and powers, which left to their own devices would never be developed in a man of a mechanical nature; they are properties that would remain dormant and be thought of as a pure fiction from a flight of the imagination.

As we observe him, mankind neither progresses, nor evolves. What would appear to be progress or 'evolution' would be found to be no more than a partial modification, which is also counterbalanced by an equivalent modification in the opposite direction. This fact can be likened to the eastern symbol that delineates the yin and yang; for every action, movement or thought pattern that eventuates, nature or the divine *must* counterbalance with an equal and opposite force in the opposite direction because balance must be maintained. This is a fundamental law of the universe. If too much positive energy or force will appear in one area, an equal amount of negative energy will then appear to maintain an equilibrium.

The evolution of mankind, as it now stands, has been greatly hampered by the fact that human beings seem to be of the opinion that forward movement may be achieved by the propagation of various theories which will appear on a regular basis.

A theory is invented and then another will present a different theory which contradicts the first and both expect that everyone will follow them. Since man is so mechanical many people do in fact believe either one theory or the other. Thus mankind becomes no more than a tool in the hands of various forces at work in the world.

The theories that do occasionally appear usually seek support for general welfare and certainly an amount of equality for all men and women, but it must be understood that the earth is not structured for that to occur. All beings are at differing levels of their soul's journey and do require vastly differing circumstances in order to experience what they need to experience. It is important to remember in the light of this that compassion is vital.

It is easy to observe as we go through life and this is something I observed while driving around as a handyman, that people are often on automatic pilot and incapable of keeping a single thought in their head for more than ten seconds. No doubt it is why they drive as badly as they do at times; cutting across lanes because they have just remembered they need to be somewhere else.

Evolution requires a level of awareness. Unless human beings can move beyond their mechanical or instinctive nature they cannot evolve. Or rather, they will not evolve very much without becoming consciously present. They sleep a slumber far more dangerous than that which is experienced at night and their senses are equally dulled.

To evolve it is vital to establish a central core, or grounded Self within. As I have mentioned the endocrine system consists of our seven Chakras; which are in actual fact organs that act as receivers and transmitters of energy to and from the divine.

'Man' as you see him on the street, as often as
not has no central and permanent 'I' that acts as
a controlling influence and is unchangeable. Every
thought, every mood, every desire, every sensation
that passes through his countenance is erroneously
labelled as an 'I' and man's entire being is most often
controlled by separate and often opposing 'I's; each
one arising from a differing portion or control centre
of the entire being.

If you consider the ramifications of having
several control centres, or combinations of more than
one centre in control, there are literally thousands
of combinations of an 'I' that can occur. Each
moment we think 'I' there is a constant struggle for
supremacy of 'I's within us. The continual alternation
and resultant conflict within has no end to it and
ultimately results in man being at the mercy of any
and all external influences. His reactions to these
external influences are no more than mechanical
repetitions of his past reactions. As a result man
cannot actually 'do' anything or react to anything
in a way that departs from his previous 'programmed'
behaviour until he becomes aware of his true state.
When he sees that he lives within a prison of his own

making he becomes able to free himself from it. Until that time even though he may think he is aware it is a superficial awareness only because it is not sourced from a central unified core within him because as yet none exists. The competing 'I's' will have him or her 'living' through a succession of imaginings; at the push and pull of feelings and programmed thoughts and reactions; subject to emotions which create the energy, often negative, which will inexorably return to impact his or her life.

At this very moment the earth itself is evolving. Few have understood that the very earth we inhabit is literally a 'conscious being.' There is consciousness even within the elements that are found surrounding the earth. Native Americans are well aware that it is possible to summon the wind and the rain and it has not gone unnoticed that there has been a decided increase in the amount of tsunamis and seismic activity on the planet since the early nineties, when the earth entered a gigantic photon belt in space.

This is not accidental; all is in accord with the wishes of the divine and the planetary cycles created by it.

Chapter Four

CATEGORIES OF MAN

feel it necessary to slightly illuminate the term 'Man', any one wishing to know fully the extent of the prison within which we find ourselves, must first understand What they are in the first place; man as he imagines himself to be is an illusion, a myth. Any effort to evolve to a higher spiritual level and acquire 'real' knowledge requires that certain things must be understood.

Humans as you observe them on the street can be placed in three main categories, man number one say, is a person whose center of gravity, or his approach to life, is centered in his base chakra a place that typifies a strong connection to the physical plane, he will rely on his physical body and his automatic instincts and reflexes outweigh his emotions and his intellect.

Man number two is on a similar level of development save for the fact that this man deals with and reacts to the world in a manner based in his emotional center, this man knows only the things he likes about the world, and also the things he does not like, should this man require a psychologist he will become fixated only on the things he doesn't like.

Man number three on the other hand, is someone that reacts to all things that occur with his intellect, this man bases his reactions on subjective, logical thinking, a man that praises knowledge above his emotions and any physical endeavors that he may observe, this may lead to him becoming an academic.

All men born to the earth, will be born into one of these three categories, Escape however, is only possible firstly after a man has realized that he is limited As I have, man number four cannot appear on the earth ready made, growth beyond one, two, and three can only occur after a man or woman comes into contact with a school of a mystical nature, man number four can only escape his prison, with the help of a teacher, or a master, people that may be known in a literal sense as men number five, six, and seven, wherein all mysteries are known and growth of the spiritual level may then be raised permanently.

As my life flowed on I occasioned more injuries to my knees. I am still unaware of the certainty of the cause but I understand that knees often demonstrate referred pain from the hips. I recall when I was approximately ten years old that on a dare I jumped off the roof of the family home and this may have been the cause or at least a contributing factor.

I have since learned that knee injuries can be created to reflect inflexibility in some areas of our lives. I had had two arthroscopies by that point but I was not aware enough to look within myself for the reasons. I just knew that it was a problem for my Aikido training.

My two girls were growing up and beginning to establish themselves in the world. In my later thirties, I would often ferry them around to their friends for their various social engagements. Taz being older was already seeing boys but Leah was not quite at that stage yet. She did however gravitate to a girl friend that was later to be found to be less than a suitable role model. I suspect that some type of drugs were being experimented with and we were not at all happy with that friendship. But Leah was the sort of person who would listen to all you had to say but in the end she would end up doing what she wanted anyway. It was time which became the teacher and eventually Leah learned that her friend did not make for a healthy relationship. We were greatly relieved as every parent would understand.

As marriages go mine was not so bad. Susan and I had gotten to know each other pretty well and had settled into a relationship of habit as much as anything. Many marriages do end up like this. My inability to connect with my inner feelings couldn't help but take a toll unfortunately.

I was still letting Susan make all the decisions about our family and our social lives and I continued to be uneasy and aloof at gatherings involving large groups of people for fear of letting people get close to me. I had learned much about how the universe actually works but still it was only an intellectual knowing, and the intellect was not where my own problem was. I was by now extremely aware of the people around me and their motivations became blatantly obvious to me but still I had no access to a heart or any emotion that I could demonstrate.

Curiously, this did not affect my love for my children. I will at this point go out on a limb and assume that all my children were souls reconnecting with me from previous lives.

Probably my lack of ability to connect emotionally to Susan was a contributing factor that would drive a wedge between us as it ultimately did. Mind you I was still of the opinion that I loved her. I suppose it was because in that life I had never had anything else to compare it with. But I was aware that Susan had a need to be in control in the house and this I tolerated because I did not at that point have any idea who the hell I was or what I wanted from life.

No doubt Susan inherited a need to be in control from her father who had, in her younger days, ruled over her with an iron hand.

People, in their ignorance, believe what they are conditioned to believe and behave the way they have observed behaviour in others and their likes and dislikes also are absorbed on a subliminal and imperceptible level.

I do not assign any blame here whatsoever, but I note that the word 'choice' is grossly misunderstood and mostly used in error. In the main, people choose only what they have been taught to choose and think the way they have been taught to think and feel, and this is the process within which we find ourselves. What you do about it is up to you. Now that I've been made more than fully aware of the process I choose the evolution option. It is my belief that the uninitiated, when all is considered, are no better off than a prisoner serving hundreds of consecutive life sentences on a prison called earth.

It is my belief that without evolution however, there exists in the universe an automatic process of degeneration – entropy – which applies to all things, solar systems, suns, and even our individual atoms which either develop or decay.

That which cannot consciously evolve will only degenerate, and this degeneration occurs mechanically also. For most people, even those that assume they are 'educated' and 'thinking' people, the single biggest obstacle to a higher awareness or consciousness is the belief that they already posses it.

We are all creations of our upbringing and our ability to gain greater awareness will be influenced by our childhood experiences.

My parents seemed unable to express love. I cannot recall them ever saying they loved me. No doubt they had their own wounds and their own problems which is possibly why my mother developed a problem with alcohol when I was in my late teens. She had grown up in an unhappy, argumentative household from what I can gather. Beatings were commonplace and living in such an emotional cauldron caused her to believe that emotions and anger had to be kept within at all cost.

She was also a woman who, being a perfectionist, had a constant fear of being judged and found to be less than adequate. She would, many times after an outing return home and speak critically about the people she had just been with, but never have the strength of character to actually say it to their faces. Expressing her feelings to the person's face would have been for her an obstacle of insurmountable terror; her inner truth being perpetually withheld.

My father was also in need of help in his own way. If at his funeral one were to walk amongst those gathered, you would hear nothing but praise regarding the type of man he was and there is no doubt there would be good cause for this, but I of course saw other sides. I suspect that my father was spoiled as a child. I don't know much about his early life but I do know this, not once in his entire life, did I ever witness him speak his own truth. He had a tendency to mock everything, no matter the topic. He would use humour to divert attention away from the subject at hand; this occurred without fail.

This was his way of hiding from his own truth, and his own fears about the world, or more precisely his own emotions. My father was, like me, uncomfortable with either displaying emotion or knowing what the hell it was that he felt at any particular moment, so his hiding place was humour. In fact the only emotion that he was ever able to connect to was his anger. Most of his life (that I observed) became a life of never fully liking who he was. This fate I also shared ... not completely unexpectedly.

In his younger years he was drawn to music and in fact was schooled in the conservatorium of music in Sydney. By the time I started growing up it was obvious to me that he was able to play many instruments with great proficiency, but as time went on it dawned on me that although he had a day job, his only opportunity to play his music (which I'd have to say that he truly loved) came when he, of a Friday or Saturday night played with two friends at wedding receptions and social functions.

I feel a sadness for him at this point. Knowing the ways of the universe as I now do I knew that any success we achieve on earth only comes to us if we truly believe that we deserve it. I also know that my father would have been given a chance at some point in his life to escape his position,

It is not, 'have I got a chance but more often; 'Have I seen my chance?' or 'do I believe in myself?'

It was also apparent that after a bad day at work my father's dislike of himself would invariably be taken out on his children. Unfortunately, at that time the leather strap was his answer to his noisy boys and that is a pain that you don't really ever forget.

Much later in life I began to understand all that happens and why and I could see that was just his conditioning. It was all he knew and all he could understand. Later on he would pay a severe price for the lack of his own evolution. By the end of his life he had had both hip joints replaced (not moving forward in life) and one knee joint (inflexibility).

Parents, who cannot express emotion, raise children who cannot express themselves emotionally. To this day my brothers and I are only able to communicate our inner truths and feelings when liberal amounts of alcohol are applied and even then my brothers fall back into old habits and tend to make light of the more serious issues, as did my father. My mother on the other hand, due to her own inability to face up to what she was feeling and express it honestly and openly, developed an ability to sidestep what was lacking in her and compensated by believing (subconsciously) that she could maintain an illusion of being in control of her life and her children by interrogation of varying types.

Her questions never seemed to end: Where were we going? Who was going to be there? How long would it take? Were they nice people? Etc.

The end result of this type of 'grilling' turned my brothers and I into people who, once the apron strings had been cut, would be reluctant to engage in too much conversation with our mother at all. We would impart as little information to her as was possible and we were reluctant to even do that. Many people outside the family unit always remark on how quiet we all are. This unfortunately was a fate my father suffered as well. But it was something we came to use as a defence mechanism.

I might add at this juncture that the role of 'interrogator' arises because these types of people, when children, growing in an environment of turmoil or hardship, or emotional upheaval, resort to various forms of deception to obtain what they think they need. This is a survival response common to children. In this case I speak of what is presumed to be 'Love' by the child, and this is obtained by (as James Redfield has already noted) four main types of tools that the child learns to use in order to receive what is assumed to be 'Love' from other people, but in actual fact is often nothing more than 'attention'.

Here again I ask you to note that whenever your attention is directed at another, energy flies from your own aura into theirs, thereby temporarily giving them the illusion of completeness that they feel they are lacking. Some people tend to be rather 'aggressive' in their attitude, demanding your attention, usually through creating fear within you. Another might choose to adopt the role of 'the aloof' demanding attention by way of playing the role of a bystander and not actively joining in the conversation around them. And let us not forget the 'poor me' who will delight in relating all of the negative events that have befallen them and thereby assuming the role of 'victim.' These types of people will usually end up creating more trouble for themselves by virtue of the fact that negative energy can only attract more negative energy.

Observe clearly what a man is doing, do not view him through the eyes of the ego, only then will you be in a position to see what he is really doing, and what he requires of you, and if you are in fact prepared to give it to him or her.

Chapter Five

THE UNIVERSE SETS
ME FREE

had become aware while working at the ABC that I had a certain amount of creative ability. I believe this has something to do with being born Aries. In fact one day in the studio it was noted that there were seventeen people in that place at that time that were Aries by birth sign.

But unfortunately I could never get management to move me to a more creative environment. My need for creative fulfilment or expression became greater the more my marriage deteriorated. Our physical relationship was not fulfilling and we were moving farther apart.

My wife was doing the best she could with her life and her conditioning but there were occasions that made it obvious that she was losing respect for me; sometimes demonstrating it publicly much to my dismay. So all in all the 'magic' was fast dissolving. Not only did she not believe in me, but I also never got to believe in myself thanks to my own conditioning. That would only come to me much later.

I was still learning and reading all I could about the universe, or what was running the universe and occasionally Susan would comment on some of the aspects found within my books but she was not greatly interested in the topic.

I don't think she believed in God but then to believe in God we have to be prepared to let go, to accept we are not in control and some people cannot do that.

Whatever the reasons there were many things drawing us apart and in the end the relationship was destined to fail. I am the first to admit that my indulgences with alcohol were a minor factor but also my ill-defined quest for gaining real knowledge of the truth of all things, which I pursued relentlessly, perhaps obsessively, could only drive us further apart.

In my own defence, if defence is at all necessary, I will say this: we live at a crucial time for the earth. It is a period that occurs only once every 26,000 years and it is a time of a great rising of the consciousness of the entire planet. This why there is increased seismic activity. Each of us has elected to be here for this turmoil; to experience it and to grow as a result of it.

My life up to that point had not been one of great success. In fact it was one of hardship and uncertainty, one of searching for a part of myself that largely remained intangible and continued to elude me. But I knew that in the end my soul had had asked to be put through that apparently fruitless search for an identity and my family likewise had elected to play a part in it as well.

So although I can apologize to my wife, she got precisely what she had come to experience on earth since most of our lives are predetermined and viewed prior to our arrival.

And all this time, my girls were growing up – much to my dismay. Taz was living away from home as young people do when they wish to spread their wings and Leah was just about to move out to live with her boy friend. Dane was still living at home. I still recall how lucky I was to have had such fortune with my children, I recall each and every moment of their lives with pride and give thanks.

But as time wore on my inner feelings about Susan and her feelings about me took a toll. We were growing apart and after some time I found it more convenient to sleep in separate rooms which I suppose was the beginning of the end of our marriage. My quest was consuming me. My lack of an adequate sexual life created much unspoken resentment within me. I ask you at this point to note that the universe has in place a method of identifying what any individual person is lacking in their makeup and this system works surprisingly well if you're aware enough to observe it.

The people that surround each of us, if you are aware enough, will reflect back your own characteristics. If you come across nothing but angry people all day, you must ask yourself what are 'you' angry about? The universe is just showing you yourself.

So ultimately God had placed me in a situation with a wife that, like me, had an inability to connect with her own inner feelings. She suffered from my own complaint; she couldn't connect with her own heart and express her own emotions. So in the end we both were never able to express what we felt and talk over our issues with each other and the union had no chance of survival; it was not meant to.

But given the knowledge I was to gain in the future I can now see that we were never meant to live out that relationship to its natural conclusion. It was not part of my soul's plan.

It is notable though, that after our separation, I did not ever consider that the universe had certain requirements that I had to fulfil. After a couple of years had passed, I would periodically have certain dreams about Susan, unsettling dreams, largely concerned with her and any new boyfriends that may have entered her life. This occurred for quite some time, and always had a disturbing effect on me. What occurred after a while though, was that my soul intervened... as it always does. If it isn't your soul it will be your own guides that hasten the appearance of a subtle message within your body.

In my own body a condition developed that caused me a large amount of discomfort – the iliotibial band in my leg began to play up constantly, causing much discomfort. This particular band connects the hip to the knee cap on the outside of the leg. I tolerated the pain for many months, trying every stretch and exercise I could think of, but alas it was all in vain; it persisted.

Finally in great desperation, I called Valerie a psychic in Nelson's Bay who would later become my teacher, because I just could not get the answer to this riddle. Normally spiritual people tend not to help you too much by identifying the reason for your ascension problems but thankfully she took pity on me and told me what the root of the problem was. I could not for the life of me figure out why the divine required me to divorce from my wife, but it did, that was the underlying reason for the dreams I had been having.

There was, still in existence, an energetic connection between us, an emotional strand that kept me from being able to raise my spirit higher and the result was that any problem with the hip is always concerned with us moving forward in life, and ascending, or addressing our issues. As soon as I went to a solicitor to begin proceedings the problem disappeared entirely.

My Aikido practice continued with Eino when my knees permitted and so did my questions to him, all of which helped me, as the saying goes:

'When the student is ready the teacher will appear'.
(Thankfully)

All the while I was moving closer to the
knowing that there would be a time when I must
begin to meditate. There was no way around the
truth, so occasionally when time permitted I began
to experiment with varying types of meditation.
Whenever I could, I would get away from noise
and slip into the bush.

For quite some time my awareness had been
growing. I noted when the crows sent me signs, I
could remember my dreams to a certain extent, and
many other signs became apparent to me. I must
admit I was warned about upcoming events while
driving one day and a radio story was sent by my
guides detailing how a man had lost most of his
possessions due to his recent divorce. Unfortunately
it took me unawares since my mind was elsewhere,
but before too long I was going through exactly the
same process.

It was about this period that I received my first
direct message from my guides, which was quite an
amazing experience all things considered. It happened
while I was driving away from one of my handyman

jobs. I had for a short time had thoughts that maybe I should write, but I didn't take the thoughts seriously because I had never even considered that I could write. But apparently my guides were keen for me to get the message so just as I turned a corner a voice spoke to me, but this was definitely not part of the normal internal dialogue that continues unabated in our heads. I was aware enough to be aware of my internal thoughts and this was different, the voice reverberated through my chest cavity, which I was later to discover held our emotional centre and is the place where much information is received from other dimensions. So I began to think about what the hell I could write.

Apparently for my marriage the final straw for Susan came one day after she had needed an internal examination for the colitis she suffered which is usually a symptom of unresolved subconscious childhood trauma. She had asked me to pick her up from the hospital in a smaller vehicle that we owned, but I turned up in the work van at the end of the day. I could not relate to her colitis discomfort and I couldn't see what the difference the vehicles made, but it was a huge difference apparently given subsequent events. We were hardly speaking to each other after that.

This also coincided with a painful knee I was experiencing that needed surgery. At that point I could see it was a matter of lack of support from her, so after sleeping apart for a year and not being able to relate to each other on any deeper level I asked her one day if she wanted me to move out, which she did. But as luck would have it I could do nothing about moving out while my knee was so painful.

Susan tolerated my uncomfortable presence for a time but eventually decided to move out herself with Dane and go back to live with her father. I must note here that Susan must really have been disenchanted with me. She was not close to her father and quite resented having to go back there. The most noteworthy event of that time was that on the night that she told me that she was leaving, for the first time in my life, at about forty-seven years old, I actually cried. Apparently, underneath everything I still thought that I loved her and probably I did.

The universe however played more than a little part in this situation. I came to later understand that I had sufficiently demonstrated to the universe and my soul guides that I was serious in my intention to begin the journey back home, our real home, to the truth. The mechanism for my marriage breakup was of little consequence. The only important factor was that if a man or a woman truly desires the truth of all things, no one could find the truth if they existed as one half of another person and any part of their demeanour was modified or controlled by another.

This may again allow you to make sense of the increase in divorces and marriage break ups since the early nineties. Many people, after being on the earth for many life times, begin to feel that there is a lack of fulfilment with their partner and discover that what is missing is their connection to the source of all things.

In short, I had moved from my family home when twenty-one years old straight into a marriage, as men do, choosing a carbon copy of their mothers, control being the predominant issue. I had never been able to find out who I was, what I wanted from the earth, what I would tolerate from the earth and what I would not. I did not know who I was and would never get to find out in a relationship. Not to mention the fact that most marriages and relationships are based on a karmic debt from past lives. I had owed Susan Anne that exact period of time from a previous life; karma cannot be bartered with and is inflexible so we separated in October 1999 and the house was placed on the market. My relationship with my children fortunately was relatively unaffected. The girls were just about self sufficient, and Dane had to move out with Susan because of his school age; he was entering high school.

That was a fearful time for me. I was hurt, bewildered and I would not even speak to my wife on the phone to discuss the sale of the house. I went to see my friend Eino with my tale of woe, I suppose for some support, but he had been on the spiritual path for more than twenty years and I got the impression that being psychic he would have been well aware of the break up long before it happened. What did happen though was that he mentioned that he was a member of a Quan-yin meditation group initiated by a Master called Suma Ching Hai who had followers all over the earth.

She was born in Vietnam but spent much of her adult life in Taiwan. She was brought up as a

Catholic but learned the basics of Buddhism from her grandmother. Ching Hai teaches a form of meditation using sound and light.

We began talking of the possibility of me following him to Thailand since he was headed there for a spiritual retreat to see the Master over Christmas that year. At first I was a little reluctant to commit, since I was short of funds due to my knee problem and had completed much less work. He mentioned the possibility of some initiations of new members to the Master at that time. This I considered given my consistent need to follow my heart to the truth. I suspect that he was always aware by the questions I was asking that that was the place I should be anyway. It was a bit of a rush to get a passport and organise myself but I did end up going. I guess it was time to put my money where my mouth was.

I found the whole experience a little overwhelming. I had never wanted to travel before so it was a huge thing for me to go to a country where I didn't know the language and immerse myself in a totally foreign culture.

But I did get there and most of the Master's followers were bussed straight to a Bangkok university.

I was again overwhelmed by the fact that large numbers of her followers were Asian in origin. This in itself did not worry me but culturally I found that in particular the Chinese women tended to behave in a manner that I found lacking in good manners. They would constantly mob the Master and attempt to touch her frequently. Suma Ching Hai was born in Vietnam; in the spiritual world the divine will send a Master to earth at the time that they are needed most, in the place they are needed the most, for the people that need them the most.

So on boxing day 1999, I sat with thirty other people in a room at the university and we were instructed in the manner of the meditation that the Master, after travelling through India and Asia all her life had found to be the quickest method of repaying all past karmic debt and leaving the earth for good. After my life to date, that sounded very appealing to me so I was initiated to the Master while I meditated. Initiation is a process whereby the Master is informed of the correct time and place where the potential initiates are waiting

Although the Master has only one physical earth body, in the divine planes there exist any number of manifestation bodies she may utilise to journey to the initiates and permanently link with their souls, the purpose of which is to incur onto herself all of the initiates past life karmic debt and free them forever from the earth.

Now I will admit that at that point after initiation I had no great cosmic realisations, others present did, and some even had their inner sight (the third eye) begin operating, but I had not been an angel during my life. However, I was left with two new sounds emanating from the divine that would forever be heard by my inner hearing. Jesus, having twelve apostles, would have had to initiate all of them in precisely the same manner, hence the crucifixion was the end result of taking all of the past life karma of the apostles onto himself and freeing them to continue his work on earth.

In effect, becoming a Master is the only method of escaping the earth. It is a teaching that we are not to eat meat. It is mentioned on the second page of the bible where it says we are only to care for animals, not consume them. So the price of initiation is to become vegetarian, which I have done. I do believe that the karma we incur through consuming meat ties us to the planet for hundreds of lifetimes.

In the end there are not Ten Commandments at all. Initiation requires that I live by five only:

No killing

No lying

No sexual misconduct (sex that hurts someone)

No drugs or intoxicants

No stealing

These I live by. It is not easy to do but it is the only way to move beyond the earth plane. All in all I found the retreat definitely confronting to a large degree. There were thousands of people from all over the world and my need to remain distant and not let the crowds overwhelm me continued to be a battle.

But while I was there something happened that gave me great hope that I was definitely on the right track. There were three sessions of meditation daily, morning, afternoon and night and the Master would appear on a regular basis in varying locations depending on her own need to clear herself of the karma she had absorbed from all new initiates. For an average human to clear all past life debt they might have to spend many consecutive lifetimes of suffering on earth to clear the debt, but a Master, because of their permanent connection to the divine and their much higher spiritual level, may only have to spend a few minutes or sometimes seconds in a less than comfortable place.

So in effect the Master was not available at every meditation, but at one point as she walked through the grounds with some of her minders, as usual there were crowds of followers (usually Chinese women) trying to get close to her and calling out and trying to get her attention. This again I felt was in poor taste and tended to annoy me. On either side of the path she walked through the crowd, and there were lines of followers two to three people deep all animatedly abuzz with excitement. I stood there watching her pass by and I thought to myself 'It would be nice to have some type of personal contact with her but I'm not prepared to behave like these people' ...

What happened next was quite amazing. The Master stopped dead in her tracks, turned ninety degrees to her right and walked straight up to me, reached past two people in front of me and shook my hand and then took Eino's hand next to me and shook his. She then continued on her journey. I turned to Eino and told him of my unspoken thought about the Master and he confirmed that he had had exactly the same thought at that moment. Now any Master that is powerful enough to read the thoughts of a couple of hundred people and sensitive enough to pick out the two thoughts that came from the heart (definitely not ego based as were many of the others) is a Master that deserves my attention and my respect.

Whilst at this retreat the Master spoke of an area of interest to me. I had worked out that if I was to write and since my interest was with the undeniable truths held by the Sufi's, then that is what I should write about. At the retreat the Master stated that she had a great respect for the Sufi's and their methods of connecting with God so I began at that time to work out what my story would entail. A comment from the Sufi's in relation to man's preponderance for a mechanical existence ...

O you who fear the difficulties of the road to
   annihilation –
Do not fear.
It is so easy, this road, that it may be
   travelled sleeping.

Mir Yahya Kashi

In the end the meditation at the retreat proved to be quite arduous for me.

Ultimately if one would wish to leave the earth permanently, after having all your past life karma taken from you by a Master it is still necessary to meditate for three hours daily to clear all your karma that stemmed from the life you are in. I found it difficult to meditate for lengthy periods, but my life had been such that apart from my three children there was nothing on earth that I wanted except to leave it, so I persevered to the best of my ability.

Within Sufism the importance of waking from the mechanical existence is paramount. The exercise of self-remembering I had practised earlier in my life gave me an undeniable insight into how little control we have over ourselves. We live in sleep and by and large we will eventually die in sleep. The extent of this prison and the dangers inherent therein soon alert you to the supreme difficulty required to escape it. No one can escape this gaol on their own, all efforts must be directed by someone that has already escaped the mechanisation that life on earth produces within us.

It is quite common to find a Master or a teacher
will have in his charge twelve students since this is
the ideal number to enable suitable observation of
any that may slip back into mechanical and habitual
behaviour. It is no accident that there were twelve
apostles studying under Jesus.

> *There are many trees: not all of them*
> *bear fruit.*

> *There are many fruits: not all of them*
> *may be eaten. Many, too, are the kinds of*
> *knowledge: yet not all of them are of value to*
> *men.*
>
> Jesus, son of Mary, The Book of Amu-Darya

Chapter Six

AND SO BEGINS
THE BEST AND WORST
TIMES OF MY LIFE

hile I was in Thailand I did try to call my wife and patch things a little but to no avail. In the long run the relationship was to fail as it was meant. I know I keep saying that but I do so because I needed to keep reminding myself. I was then committed to raising my spiritual level and knowing God, the real truth and my wife couldn't believe, so in the end there was no compatibility possible. We were walking in different directions.

So I returned home to Australia still not knowing what lay ahead of me. The house was on the market for the time being and I just did whatever handy man work I could. I used to call my daughters regularly to see how they were. They meant the world to me. Both were living with friends elsewhere in Sydney so I liked to call regularly to know that they were safe.

I eventually began to talk to my wife on the phone and get reports on the sale but things would never be the same again between us. It was of concern to me that Taz always seemed to be having problems with boyfriends. I used to advise her regularly on her attitude to her problems with boys, due to my ability to pick up on the underlying motivations of people, but love is what love is and you cannot control what they are feeling for someone unfortunately.

Eventually the family house sold and I had to find a place to live, I did find a townhouse elsewhere in Terrey Hills. Susan arranged a moving van and took the furniture that she required to start over her life, leaving me enough to continue on with. So I had a new address and an uncertain future ahead of me.

I had been through quite a lot in the past couple of months and was feeling lost and needing to take stock. The meditation group I found to be overly secretive and even required guards to patrol the meditation hall during the process. This was apparently to ensure the purity of the venue and not let outsiders view the process involving certain postures contained therein. I found this a little intimidating because I had always rebelled against authority figures, so it was some time before I got into a process of regular meditative practice.

As time went on I began to start writing a film script along the lines of a man that had been damaged by the hand of organised religion, namely the Christian brothers, I worked away slowly on the project for some time as per my previous instructions from my guides.

My moving coincided with Taz deciding that she would come to live with me, which I welcomed. Leah was living with a boyfriend on the south side of Sydney and working in a clothes shop in Paddington and was not able to help with the moving process. That began what was to become the best and the worst time of my life. I did not have all that much money and all that much work so I was really sweating on the money from the sale of the house arriving, Taz had moved all her things in and was working but to me she never appeared to be happy for a great length of time; there was always something bothering her and this worried me as it would any parent.

But ultimately over that period my daughter and I grew ever closer together and we became not only father and daughter but great friends as well. I now believe that Taz and I had a long and loving relationship in many past lives. As time was to testify I would have done anything for my Taryn Joy, I would have died for her. Finally though, the money from the sale of the house did arrive, which was a relief for me. Susan had asked for a sixty/forty split of the money which I agreed to so I ended up with $139,000. At that point my work van was getting quite old and I took a chance and leased a brand new one so I could keep on working. At first things went along smoothly enough and there was some work around, enough to pay the rent every week and live at least.

At about that time at the end of 2000 my son Dane was in his final year of high school and graduated with the honour of being named dux of the school; which made me very proud indeed. Taz had to work on that day but Leah, Susan and I attended with great pride.

As I said I was proud of the type of people we had raised. Taryn after various jobs working in clothing and women's shoe shops decided to undertake a part time TAFE course in business human resources to improve herself. She passed with distinctions and yet again I allowed myself a feeling of pride. Dane, before long undertook a course at Macquarie University to begin studies in finance. Leah, had expressed an interest in going to England for some reason so I would occasionally travel over to Paddington to have lunch with her. It was on one of these occasions that I decided to give her the money for her trip to England, although I didn't understand the reasons for her needing to go. I was sad to see her go.

It was the best time of my life because Taz and I were similar in our natures and our sense of humour served to complement each other. She was a wonderful person with a good heart and I loved her dearly and always will.

We laughed together often and a bond grew that would eventually transcend time and space. She would always look after herself physically; running quite often and always eating the right foods. I admired her greatly.

As time went on I began to practice my meditation at every opportunity. I was still hearing the interdimensional sounds and they grew louder as time progressed, but I tended to thirst for more prominent signs that I was achieving something, so I began to try to practice some sort of astral projection methods which I had read about. I was unsuccessful in the beginning but months later it happened quite by chance in the middle of the night, about three in the morning. I still do not know how it actually happened but my astral body floated out above my sleeping form. Apparently though it occurred at a time where my Master was performing some healing on my body.

I don't know how to fully explain that experience to you, suffice to say that I still knew who I was, and where I was, but there floating three feet above my bed was a shimmery figure with shifting patches of light changing positions on a regular basis. I had absolutely no fear at this point. One of the fringe benefits of being initiated is that you are protected from all types of harm in any and all dimensions. Some of the lower levels of the astral plane harbour some creatures that are bestial and there are other beings that may appear human but with portions of their bodies grossly misshapen and distorted. I knew that it could only have been my Master there above me. But what the experience did do was convince me that we cannot die. All my memories were there and intact; we definitely live on after we leave the body. Unfortunately the Master had not finished her work on me so she pushed my astral body back into my sleeping form. It was an experience however that could not be forgotten.

At another time while Taz was staying with her mother for a night I was awakened by a voice that called my name. There was no one in the room or elsewhere in the house. I looked outside the curtains and there was no one outside either. I was later to find out via a psychic that it was one of my guides calling me to assess my inner hearing capabilities.

As time progressed I began to get phone calls and emails from Leah in London. It cheered me up considerably to know she was fine over there, but I was always uneasy about Taz's welfare. There was an intangible sadness that I couldn't put my finger on. This was to worry me for quite some time. Already in her life she had a failed relationship with a boy that was clearly not her equal or at least, definitely not right for her.

With the love I had for her and my awareness I did my best to explain the motivations of the people around her. There were even girlfriends in her life that she had problems with at times. Taz's heart was pure and she would never have hurt a fly in her life. She was well aware of my own problems because I had explained about never bonding with anyone at my birth and my inability to feel comfortable around new people so she was always trying to get me to go out and visit the friends I did have.

The reason I love her so much is that she was the only one that did not give up on me; she stood by me, and I stood by her. Often I would, after a day's work, travel thirty minutes up to Chatswood to pick her up from work and buy her any particular food that she wanted. I will never forget our time together. She also had the uncanny ability to buy exactly the right gift for me; I still have them all to this day.

Leah had returned home for a period which was a relief. She spent some time with me thankfully but only long enough to earn more money to go back to London. This I found difficult to understand, but past a certain age you can't control their lives and I was lucky to be able to control my own.

Leah was a pleasure for me to have around, because she loved children and had infinite patience with them. She had often worked as a nanny in London.

But unfortunately as soon as she had enough money she left for London again. I couldn't understand what the attraction was. It was hard for me to see her go but I could not stop her and had no right to try.

Now right here I must mention that by becoming initiated to a Master I had declared to the universe that 'I wanted out' – I was on the ascension

There are some things about ascension you are not warned about, not the least of which is that to raise your spiritual level you of necessity must confront every fear that you have about the world. The next thing that happened was that work stopped coming to me, the phone stopped ringing. At first I was not too concerned but the situation lasted for months. Luckily I had the money from the sale of the house to fall back on but I was still very concerned about the situation.

It was quite some time before I had the realisation about why this had happened. When I was about twelve or thirteen years old I was home alone with my younger brothers while my parents were out and two policemen arrived with a summons for my father concerning an unpaid bill. Apparently my subconscious at that age worked out that, if you didn't have any money, you were a criminal – a mechanical thought if there ever was one. Once I had had that realisation about where the fear had come from things slowly returned to normal but it had cost me a lot of money paying the rent all those months.

What happened next was the beginning of the nightmare that my life became. My baby girl, my first born beautiful daughter, developed a small discolouration on her back. At first I wasn't concerned too much, but a skin specialist thought it should be removed so we took no chances and had it done. All was fine for some time and things got back to normal and Taz resumed her work after a day or so of healing. Taz kept occupied with yet another boy friend who couldn't keep his act together for any length of time. She deserved so much better than she had.

At that point I was aware after the death of Susan's mother that I had a fear of death. Olive, in retrospect, after having two strokes, simply grew tired of living with the restrictions that the strokes left her with and while in a nursing hospital yet again, made the decision to stop eating and starve herself to death.

I have great respect for Olive she was a brave woman and I love her. But my fear of death and dying ensured that I put off until the last minute my trip to the hospital to say my goodbyes to her and I subsequently arrived too late. But not too long after Olive passed away I felt a hand one night gently touch my knee. I now know beyond any doubt that it was Olive, who, able to see my fears about death, had come to forgive me while I lay awake in bed.

I would also never go to watch a film where I knew that the lead character was to die. It was 2002 and I never dreamed that I was about to undergo the most fearful journey that a parent could undertake and I will never forgive God while ever I'm on earth. Possibly when I die I will understand to a much greater extent why, but not yet.

Even having learned what I had the reality is that we still feel.

After some months Taryn developed another spot on her back, this started to concern me greatly, and my fear increased dramatically, but after both her parents having a run in with cancer I had hoped that the chances of Taz having a serious problem would be purely an unfortunate coincidence. Again the trouble spot was removed and we hoped that things were going to get back to normal. I cannot express the extent of my love for my daughter, it is infinite. I felt every second of her pain. We connected on a much deeper level than I'd ever experienced before in my life. I'm sure all parents will relate to these feelings.

Unfortunately there was much more pain to come, for all of us. Leah came back again for a short time but this was before the problems with Taz became too debilitating and always left to go back to London again. Taz kept working all the while until the process began to cause her pain most of the time. The problem spots kept on reappearing again and again over a three year period, after the first few an entire body scan was undertaken and the results were not encouraging, it was melanoma and in various places throughout her body. They began her on a series of radiotherapy sessions at regular intervals; the tumours were mainly affecting her spine and the sciatic nerve.

I was sufficiently concerned to visit a psychic to try and get some information on the outcome for my daughter, but as I mentioned the psychic was not shown the final outcome. He mentioned only that all would be well, which in the eyes of the divine, means that all is as it should be. On earth the paths we travel are written by our souls, nothing can change that. But I did have the knowledge that the mind is quite a powerful tool so I put mine to work, trying to burn the tumours out of her with a brilliant white light, I practiced this at every spare moment.

When Taz finally had to stop working, I rarely worked after that and I took her to her radiotherapy sessions and home again, and drove her wherever she needed to go. Nothing was more important than my girl. Dane had just about finished his university course and came to see Taz whenever he was able. He was a good brother to her and a good son.

There were times when Taz felt the need to stay with her mother in the home unit she had bought in Balgowlah. During these periods I spent my time still trying to burn the cancer out of her body with the white light. Wherever she was, I was. I spent most of my time with her; she was the only important thing

in my life, the only one that hadn't deserted me. I
owed my Taz. After the second year of the cancer Taz
found it extremely difficult to move around without
pain and was taking a great deal of medication to ease
it. I still had hopes of a cure of some sort appearing
and I kept my mind working on the white light.

I prayed and I meditated for some sort of miracle
but none appeared for me. I had thought that my
time with the chemotherapy chemicals was the worst
time of my life but was mistaken. Nothing else can
diminish the terror I felt for every single day of those
three years. Sometimes Taz stayed with me sometimes
with her mother; wherever she was I was, clinging
to the hope that there was some way out of this; a
miracle. Many times I recalled what the psychic had
told me and took the words as a sign that things
would turn out

Well, I was always hopeful when I was with Taz,
I never had anything but positive words for her.

Before the pain became too much for her Taz
decided that she wanted to get a Chihuahua This I
could not refuse her, so we drove out to the other side
of Sydney to look at a cute little dog she had seen
advertised. On the trip out there something occurred

that made me stop and think. A car had been double parked and was blocking the lane in front of us. I tend to get angry when I can see that people are thoughtlessly inconveniencing others through sheer laziness so I expressed a slight displeasure. My daughter said only this 'You have to take the good with the bad' in reference to life on earth.

It was at that moment my intuition told me that my Taz was light years ahead of us in her evolution on earth, it was a profound moment for me. I still didn't know what was going to happen in the end but I gladly bought the little dog for her and all the necessary equipment that one needs for the dog's maintenance.

At one point, sadly, there was a tumour in her brain that had to be removed which was done out at Westmead hospital, as were some sessions of chemotherapy that she had to undergo. My anxiety and the pain I felt for her surpassed anything I had experienced in my life. It broke my heart to see her with her head shaved and a long line of staples used to reattach the skin.

I was not capable of work and I didn't have much coming in anyway so my money began to dwindle on a regular basis, but it did not matter my time with Taz was all that did matter. In the third year of the illness she found it quite painful to move around and spent long periods in her bed. She would talk on the phone to her boy friend occasionally but she was beginning to see that he was less than adequate and began losing her feelings for him; she had more urgent needs that required attention.

If she was at her mother's home unit she was unable to walk without pain so whenever she had to go to the hospital for radiotherapy Dane and I had Taz sit on a chair and we carried her down all the steps to the car. We also borrowed a wheelchair from her grandfather which came in very handy.

Susan Anne was able to take time off her work and we both accompanied Taz as much as we could for her treatments, but by that time I needed medication to calm my nerves and to function. I felt every single pain that my daughter endured. I stopped meditating, unable to calm myself. I never stopped praying though. Heaven hears all prayers, but in the end I achieved nothing with them. I made up my mind during those three years, that I would never come back to the earth again. I do not want to be in a place where a man can feel such an intense love and then have it torn away from him. Anyone that has lost a child will know this feeling …

Leah was still in London through all this turmoil and it was difficult to get her to seriously consider returning. I was only later to understand why this was so. Eventually Taryn's illness got to the point where she couldn't even eat so we knew that yet again she had to return to the hospital. We didn't know that it was for the last time. Taryn begged us not to take her back to hospital and that broke my heart

But it was necessary because she wasn't eating much at all. Initially they placed her in a four bed ward and carried out more scans and radiotherapy for a week or so but finally her doctor called my wife and I into a separate room and admitted that there was nothing more they could do for her. A part of me was a little relieved. I had suffered as Taz had suffered and I thought she had suffered enough. Why on earth did her suffering need to be drawn out over three years? Was there no mercy left in heaven?

They then moved Taz into a single private room and mercifully began her on morphine drips which persisted for the last two weeks or so of her life. From that point on they set up an additional cot in the room and whether it was Susan or myself or Dane and Leah there was always at least one of us there with her for twenty four hours a day. But try as we might it was extremely difficult to get her to take any nourishment. We just had to allow nature to take its course. It was unbearable for me those last days; there were still portions of her hair missing from all her treatments, mercifully the morphine made sure that she was asleep just about all of the time and not really aware of much pain.

Then on the twenty first of September 2005 in her thirtieth year at ten minutes past four in the morning with all of us present Taz breathed her last, and returned to the place we all come from, and will all return to. Although I hadn't meditated for quite a while, I still retained some ability to be able to tell that there was a presence hovering above the bed. I hoped that it was either an angel or my Master waiting to carry my most special daughter to our real home. I said goodbye to her with a kiss on her forehead and one final hug.

The only thing that got me through the ordeal was that initiation comes with a guarantee that sixteen generations of your own family will be gently eased out of their body and ushered to a much, much better place than would normally occur.

Chapter Seven

SIGNS FROM A MASTER

I remember my wife noting with exclamation that Taz was born at ten minutes past four in the afternoon back in 1975; not a coincidence I suspect. But we then packed up all Taryn's possessions from the room and left the hospital for the last time just as the daylight was beginning to show. My children went with Susan in her car and I was in my work van. Speaking honestly I was still in the throes of relief that Taryn's suffering was over and so was ours; the grieving would come a little later. But I looked across at the passenger side seat where Taz had sat many, many times and I cried.

As we both pulled out of the hospital car park, although I was upset I took note of a significant sign. As we turned on to the road home there were one hundred pigeons that took flight from positions high on the hospital walls and flew away down the road.

Being used to the way the divine operates, for me that was a sign from my baby girl, she was letting me know that she was finally free; the pain and her suffering had ended. This sign was also noted by my son Dane which told me that he himself was more evolved that the rest of the family.

And then slightly later, as we travelled north over the harbour bridge, I saw that the day had started with clouds on the horizon, but as we drove north we saw a huge break in the clouds and the rising sun beamed its radiant light onto the roadway on both our cars.

Now sceptics would to a man call this nothing but a coincidence. But I knew better. My contact with my friend Eino, who during my daughter's illness had moved north up the coast to Taree had taught me much, not the least of which was that our souls are the only things in the universe that are indestructible.

Eino had begun his spiritual evolution at least twenty years before me and had become psychic long ago and had the ability to heal people. He told me while we were in Thailand during my initiation that any initiate and their families automatically get maximum protection from a Master.

The sun shining through the clouds as it did showed me that my Taz was now standing in God's light and protection. It was my Master that had played more than a small part in creating those signs for us at my daughter's request.

My cousin Diane had come down from Newcastle to try and support me during this process thank goodness, so I arrived back home and fell into her arms. At that point I was exhausted and then slept uneasily for the rest of the day. The pain that the loss created was unbearable and I required calming medication for some time, especially at the funeral. I prepared some words to describe what I was feeling and fortunately Leah volunteered to read the piece for me because I just couldn't do it. My attachment to Taz was the most significant emotion I had ever experienced and ever would.

My cousin Diane was also spiritual and had started her own journey early in the 1990's. She was a huge help to me when I needed it and tried to explain how the situation could be made sense of in view of the ultimate purposes of the divine. This is yet another example of the extent of the manipulation by the divine and the placement of certain people we need to come into contact with, but while there may have been a greater divine purpose, all I knew was pain.

I did have a little work to do but the time I spent looking after Taz had dwindled what was left of my money and I also paid for the funeral; that I did gladly. I kept on working whenever I could but there were many periods of overwhelming grief where I had to just stop and cry by the side of the road and this was to continue for a few years.

My awareness of the world around me was intense. About two days after the funeral I was sitting at McDonalds with my cousin having a drink when I was again amazed with yet another sign from my daughter. Outside at the exterior tables on the external speakers a song played which made the hairs on my neck stand up. Queen had recorded a song called: 'You are my best friend.'

It began to play. You can't, unless you have done some meditation be aware of what a 'knowing' is, it is a term used to describe how your intuition tells you that you must pay attention to this.

I don't know how much power is available to our souls on the other side but I knew beyond any doubt whatsoever that Taz had arranged for that song to play to let me know how much she loved me. Unfortunately it made my grief return immediately and I had to head for the van and make way for more tears.

My cousin eventually went back home and I then proceeded to return to my handyman work whenever it came to me. I was grieving most days. After my cousin left I felt the need to call Eino in Taree. He could tell how upset I was and confirmed that my daughter was safe with our Master and free of the earth and its problems. After the signs I had received I knew that it was true, our hearts are connected for all time. I was aware that our souls can hear us and know what we are thinking and during the preceding couple of years Taz was aware of the fact that I had to write and that I meditated often. But there was a time when a new song was released on the radio called 'Take me out' by Franz Ferdinand, I had previously remarked to Taz that it would be perfect to use in the film I was writing.

I kept talking to Taz frequently, positive she could hear me, mostly while driving the work van around. I asked her questions in between my periods of grief and I found that she was able to answer me. When I needed to ask her something I turned on the car radio and found the 'Take me out' song started playing, this happened many times, too many times to be coincidence. She could see how lost I was without her and when I asked her if she thought I should get a dog, I turned on the radio to hear the first couple of bars of one song begin, only to be stopped and 'Take me out' then suddenly began. This gave me great confidence that we would both meet again.

I had, on the advice of my doctor, gone to see a psychologist to see if she could be of use in the healing process but the psychologist admitted that I was too aware of the process for her to be of any help to me. It was a matter of feeling the emotions as they rose up; no one could shorten the process.

It was only with the help of Eino and Diane that I then began to understand the inner workings of the universe. I would be grieving for some time to come but bit by bit everything fell into place; there really was no death.

Taz had had a miserable life on earth; she frequently had problems with boyfriends and some of her girlfriends. Susan remarked after the funeral that our Taz had had a 'shit of a life'. This I had picked up on during that wonderful period we were together, there were many times when she would withdraw into herself and I could feel an underlying sadness in her energy that I couldn't shake loose without a tremendous effort. Eino had later remarked after I went up to visit him that suffering clears karmic debt. This I knew came directly from his own soul guides in an attempt to ease my pain and make me realise what was actually happening and why.

If a man, a man whose soul was tired after countless incarnations on earth, a man that had never bonded with anyone in his life, except in a most superficial manner and had built up an impenetrable wall around his heart and would not allow anyone to ever hurt him, how would God deal with this situation?

Firstly God would send someone to the earth that the man could not help but love, someone whose appearance in one of the man's past lives would immediately ensure an instant connection and an unwavering recognition of a strong bond by virtue of that person's familiar soul energy. And when that man was ready, and had declared his need to find the truth of all things, God would then tear that person away from him, not in a merciful instant death but in a deliberate slow process that would, little by little, allow that man to increase what he was feeling in his heart, until ultimately in the end there was no longer a wall around his heart, until that wall was shattered into a million fragments.

This is what I believe. Trust me, when I say, there is no greater pain than losing a child. It is easier to die yourself than watching your own child die in front of you. You will never leave that pain behind you no matter how long you live.

My Taz had come to earth to show me what unconditional love really is, to make me feel for the first time in my life and to know what real love is. On earth love is a mere fraction of what we are to feel in our real home. I was to cry daily for quite some time. Never had I felt so deeply, nor would I ever again. But I continued to write the film script whenever I was able to describe in metaphor form what had happened to us and why.

Chapter Eight

MIRRORS

y period of mourning was never really to end. My past life connection to Taz was clearly a deep connection, as was its purpose in the eyes of the divine.

Whenever I could I talked to my daughter, knowing that she could hear me, but eventually the radio stations took 'Take me out' off the current play lists so I became saddened because I was unable to get replies from her. The very first thing I did after the cremation was to go and pick up her ashes; at that point I needed to be near her in whatever capacity I could, in my ignorance at that time I just needed to hold her.

I was vaguely aware of why it had happened, that some souls volunteer to come back here specifically to die at an early age to assist other souls to experience growth and that from my daughter's point of view her ultimate purpose apart from helping me was to clear, by way of her suffering, a lot of her karmic debt, but my bitterness remained intact.

My handyman work was slowing up markedly and after some time I wondered why. My finances were by then quite meagre and I decided that perhaps I should go back to live with my elderly parents since the rent was quite expensive where I was. I thought about this at length. Their unit was quite small and less than comfortable so I wasn't looking forward to it so I asked for some sort of guidance as to what I should do. I received my answer by way of a sign from a crow.

As I sat out in front of the unit a crow came and landed on a tree right outside the unit. This was a positive sign all things considered, so I had all my possessions put into storage and moved in with them. I had no choice really, all the time I had spent with Taz during her illness had depleted most of my money but I wouldn't have given up one single second of the time I spent with her.

I was initially unaware of the underlying reasons for this change of address. I set myself up in their spare room and things were adequate for a brief time but it soon became apparent that my mother and

I were not to get along. I had learned too much about people's motivations and her flaws became transparent to me. She was a woman that needed to be in control and at fifty years of age I had formed my own view of the universe and life, in addition to which I was still mourning my daughter. Basically she annoyed the hell out of me.

It was a reminder that on a spiritual path the learning never stops; there is always more to learn and to grow from, if you are aware enough everyone is your teacher. If we fail to walk the path our souls have chosen for us, or fail to deal with our inner issues, pain will inevitably result.

My father had already had one of his hips replaced and one knee that was soon going to need it as well. Our souls reside within our chest cavity close to our hearts, right up against our spines and able to affect every nerve that runs through our bodies.

If we fail to walk the path chosen by the soul or fail to deal with any of the issues, it will correspond by alerting us by causing a difficulty somewhere in our bodies, if not pain, to alert us. Unfortunately the medical profession remain largely unaware of these connections. Science-based medical professionals are not quite aware of the soul or even where it might reside in the body. Any problem that tends to reappear in the body should be viewed as a message, an important message. I've experienced this myself during my spiritual apprenticeship. In the beginning it will begin as a musculature pain or sore tendon or the like, but as time goes by the soul, if the message is ignored, and there is always an underlying spiritual cause for the message, will take the discomfort up to the next level and arthritis perhaps will make its presence felt. Ultimately if the issues are ignored and never addressed, a joint will need replacing.

If you truly wish to know yourself, observe your parents, they are your greatest mirrors. The universe has been constructed in such a manner to show each of us who we really are.

In fact since all our souls are vibrating much faster than our bodies all your relationships are your mirror. What are your friends showing you about yourself that you are unable to see clearly. What do your parents and friends fear? Are they your fears?

I suspect that my mother played a great part in controlling but not supporting my father during his life. That and his inability to be able to speak his own truth and discuss what he really thought about life and other people.

It became apparent that he did love my mother when all was said and done, although at one time he did demonstrate some indiscretion with another woman, so perhaps all was not as rosy as it may have appeared.

And in truth, I do not know how that affected my mother but it must have been traumatic.

The path that I had chosen to follow, the road to ascension, is not an easy one, at least not for me. It can be a long, tiresome undertaking with many twists turns and dead-ends. The divine will present you with every single fear that you have, perhaps more than once if the message is not clearly understood. You will be tested, dependent upon how many fears you do have ingrained within you.

As I said my mother needed to keep asking questions of her children, using this as a means of obtaining energy from others and to a lesser extent to maintain a feeling of being in control of her life and us, through obtaining more information. It was an illusion that she would never release.

There were aspects of my mother's nature that were unkind. She had a tendency to criticise others behind their backs. Perhaps it made her feel stronger. As I grew I became aware that she had an intense fear of being judged as less than perfect. When talking to anyone new, she would always present herself as a virtual angel, always in the most positive light although that is perhaps not unusual in this world and no doubt there are many like her.

There was a level of hypocrisy about it all and it was only later in life that she revealed more of her true self. She was living with my brother and his wife and he, like I, had chosen to marry a woman like his mother. There were then two women who needed to be in control.

In fact each of us married wives that my mother ended up alienating because of her inability to see her four sons as anything less than perfection in motion. There are no perfect people on the earth, but my mother saw her four sons as God's gift to the world. She was totally out of touch with any form of reality at least in regard to her children.

Within us there is, shall we say, a silent observer and to avoid confusion we may call it the subconscious for the time being. The silent observer within my mother was well aware of my mother's habits and ultimately she paid a price for her own failings. The message was received by her soul and she ultimately developed a case of macular degeneration, which reduced her eyesight to about forty percent in one eye only, the underlying message being that my mother inwardly knew what kind of person she was and it contributed to her diminished eyesight. Symbolically, she did not want to look at what kind of person she was, too closely.

My pain at that time was such that I just wanted to be left alone, but that wasn't to be. There were always questions, an endless tirade requiring me to pay her more attention. When I wasn't writing my film script I had to install my own television in my room just to remove myself from her constant arrival at my door with yet another question or an attempt to change my thinking in some way. But after our childhood my brothers and I had learned that saying as little as possible to her was the only place to hide. My stay there was severe enough for me to stay away from them as much as possible. Even my meditation had to be carried out in public parks and other areas that allowed an amount of relative privacy. I hated every minute of my time there.

I eventually worked out why I had been told to go there in the first place. A person couldn't know him or herself without having a comprehensive knowledge of where they have come from. In other words the universe was telling me to have an intense look at my parents first hand, in an effort to examine my own conditioning.

This was the only way I could ever fully appreciate what within me, needed to be changed. My father was I suppose kind of harmless apart from the inability to speak his inner truth and letting my mother control his life and make all the decisions. But my mother I saw, had huge problems, with a negative attitude towards life. No matter what situation she was presented with, her conditioning led her to only be able to see a negative outcome and this had her in a perpetual state of stress, worry and anxiety.

This, considering where I wanted to end up, trying to raise my spiritual level, was wholly unacceptable. Negative energy begets more negative energy; my time there was a torture. I could only cope with my mother with my daughter's ashes close by and held them tightly to me nightly while I cried. It was a nightmare for me, but a necessary one.

One thing that arose in my awareness though, was the extent to which I was unable to connect to them in any form. While I was there I was perfectly honest with my mother and told her that I did not feel a connection to her, or any type of love at all, but she was unable to accept that what she had failed to do on the day I was born, had consequences. She was then at her age, finally able to say 'I love you' to me continually as was my father but the wall around my heart was still very much in place, and I was appalled at her attempts to hug me and get closer to me. She was baffled and couldn't understand why I couldn't have any feelings for her.

My relationship with my mother was a part of my journey of learning and growing.

Bit by bit pieces of my own puzzle began to fall into place during my stay there, albeit slower than I would have liked. Although my father had built the family home we grew up in, by the time I was in early high school, with three brothers, there was much pushing and shoving going on. It was no more than a simple fibro house, but my brothers and I had done much damage to the interior plaster walls and to be honest I mostly felt embarrassed to ask friends around there. I felt that way for many years. My father, after having built the house, I noted, was reluctant to ever repair the damage we boys had done or try to repaint the damage. He was, as I have experienced later in my own life, 'burnt out' and past it; the earth was too hard for him.

In addition to which, after having many jobs in his life, none of which were significant earners, there was never enough spare money to repair the house anyway. I did notice though that he always found sufficient money to enable him to buy whatever musical instrument he was currently enamoured with and it was clear he truly loved his music. The regular practice was something he carried on right up to the end of his life. He was a man with a good heart underneath all else. I recall from when I was quite young, during a family outing close to the Haymarket, we walked by a drunk man that had just been thrown out of a pub, and was unable to even stand, he was lying in the gutter. My father stopped and took the man's hat, gently raised the man's head and put the hat under him so he would not hurt his head on the gutter when he awoke.

Life for both my parents I saw was difficult. Both required second jobs to make ends meet and feed us. Unfortunately though they were both emotionally limited and never able to say 'I love you' to us, this we all needed to hear but it never came at the times we needed it, only years later when it was too late.

I observe here that Susan Anne suffered from my own problem and reflected back my own lack of emotion. What did happen though was that my parents were so out of contact with their own emotions that they compensated by buying us gifts as a form of love. They went out of their way to give us exactly what we wanted at birthdays and Christmas, but in the end, this can only have the effect of creating within us a belief that we are a little 'special' and that the world owes us something. They could not have done us any greater damage.

It had the effect of conditioning in us, the view that the things that we wanted in life would come to us, rather than my brothers and I venturing out into the world and working for what we wanted. In addition, my father I became aware, had an inner conditioning that had him believing that he was unworthy of any great success in life and that life was a struggle and that was exactly what he created. His own mother also had a belief that boys were of greater significance in the world, and treated him as being 'special'.

My own mother was always at odds with my father's mother, which represents a mirror reflection of 'control' being the basic issue; referring to my grandmother as a 'witch' more than once. My father, in respect to her comments about his own mother over the period of his life, learned as we boys had, to remain silent and for all intents, hidden. He managed to foster the ability to nod or make non-committal statements rather than have to say what he actually thought about the current topic of my mother's tirade.

I find it difficult to adequately describe the depths of my mother's negativity towards life but I know it impacted me profoundly and more so before I became aware enough to 'see' it. I am unable to recall anything positive that she has ever said about what was happening around her. She would be always expecting something to go wrong or someone to get hurt at any point. Unfortunately this particular trait was passed on to all her sons. This was one reason in particular that I was engineered into returning there to observe her first hand.

It was not until much later that I became aware of the effects of negativity on our lives; the effect is to say the least dramatic. As time went on and my own spiritual level increased, the rate at which my body was vibrating began to steadily rise. At first the effects are easy to dismiss, a dropped and broken glass here, dropping tools in an awkward to get at space, a slight dent in the van I worked in, and many other instances that at first you would ignore,

But at first what appeared to be an accident, after my awareness grew, I was able to recognise that these 'incidents' occurred immediately after a negative thought, or emotion had passed through my mind or emotional centre.

Here I will make a distinction between our hearts and our emotional centre. The emotional centre can be thought of a system of nerves that runs across our upper chest regions and can be activated by the brain or even the ego at other times. The necessity of me living back with my parents became not only a financial issue; it was an imperative for further growth in me.

Which reminds me, as we all need to remind ourselves, that we choose our lives and our experiences.

Thinking about the parents I had chosen explained much for me. I recalled once that after receiving an amount of money for a job, I sabotaged myself by forthwith reversing the van into my own pushbike and smashing the rear windscreen. Our conditioning is slow and occurs in a subtle and insidious manner, such is the design of the universe and would explain to an extent why some of us actually need reincarnation; ascension cannot be achieved in one life only.

But while I was at my mother's house I used to search frequently on the Internet to try and get more information about what Taz might be experiencing on the other side of our existence. Since I could no longer hear our 'song' on the radio I was trying to find other ways to make contact. But apparently Taz hadn't finished communicating with me. One day during a search I looked up a page dealing with other peoples communications with their passed loved ones, and there across the top of the page, in a large font size, in red ink, was the sentence:

'STOP HUGGING MY ASHES
THEY'RE NO LONGER ME.'

Taz was right of course. I recalled my own astral experience and the fact that I had full awareness of who I was and where I was while my body was still asleep underneath me, so I took her point, the part of my daughter that was the most real was in another dimension.

I remained in contact with my cousin Diane during my time living with my mother and I had asked her if she knew of any good psychics up in the Newcastle area. As a parent I wanted more information about my Taz. Diane gave me two possible numbers in her area, one of which was three hours drive away, but since Diane highly recommended her, that is where I went.

By this time Leah had again left for London and Dane had started a job in finance in Sydney. Susan it appeared had very little wish to contact me so I eagerly set off to Nelson Bay for my first meeting with a wonderful lady named Valerie; a psychic, a

medium and a councillor. During my first meeting
with her, I was extremely nervous, which she was
aware of and tried to put me at ease, but I was so
glad that I went. Valerie recorded the reading and I
still have the tape. My Taz was aware of how much
I missed her and why I was going and her messages
through Valerie rang very true. I knew in my heart
that it was my Taz.

Valerie almost immediately felt that someone on
'the other side' wanted to communicate with me and
she asked whom it might be. I told her my story and
she confirmed that yes it was my Taz and she added
that Taz's death appeared to be sudden, which was
quite true since the last two weeks of her life Taz was
sleeping because of the constant morphine drip and
was unaware of what was happening to her. Valerie
was a good psychic and medium. I was so lucky to
have found her. She was a firm believer in spirituality
being heart based, and was very sensitive to the pain
I was feeling before I had even mentioned it.

Taz relieved my anxiety by telling me that she
was quite happy there, and felt a little cheated
by the earth and God by taking her far too soon.
Valerie explained that she could feel in my daughter

and myself a great deal of emotion and a need to reconnect with each other. Taz had wanted to spend many more years with me, and I with her, but apparently God always wins or, as I said before, our destiny is written.

Valerie also noted that because I was undergoing such hardship by way of my mother's attempts to control my thinking and my life, my daughter said I needed to let go of the pain my mother was creating in me. I was to discover that during the lonely unhappy nights spent at my parents, after holding tightly to her ashes at bed time, my Taz came to me every night while I slept to heal the pain I had felt from that day. As I said, our connection was extremely deep.

But during that visit with Valerie, my daughter more that once stated how much she loved me and how good I was as a father. Bless her. But there was more information that Valerie had to impart to me.

I had had a dream 'sent' to me one night by my guides, a dream within which I was travelling around the state with a doctor gaining knowledge of his trade. At the time I thought nothing more about it and took no notice of it, but Valerie was shown that that indeed was my task on earth; I was to be a Reiki healer. This I didn't seriously consider at the time since my primary concern was the wellbeing of my daughter.

But that day I gained a great deal of confidence in Valerie and a new respect for heart based love. My daughter, through Valerie asked that I continue to communicate with her because she still needed to feel connected to me, which I did on a daily basis anyway and write my feeling toward her regularly. There would come a time stated Valerie, once my own healing had occurred and the pain had gone, due to my constant meditation I would be able to place my hands on my own heart and communicate readily with Taz. This gave me great hope for the future and an even greater motivation to meditate daily; even some days, for four hours or so.

I finally did reach that point; the heart is the one organ that connects us all, but you must first understand what love is and immerse yourself in it regularly. I have observed that on earth that which passes for love is often more aptly described as a 'need'.

All in all Valerie was to give me more good news on that first visit. Olive, my mother in law, who had died some time before I had been initiated in Thailand was always with and cared for my daughter, which was a great relief for me, since I was still feeling some guilt about my weakness and inability to visit her on her deathbed.

I left Valerie that day more than elated after connecting with my daughter, and it was the beginning of a friendship that still exists today. Every time I wanted to communicate with Taryn I would drive up there to get an update through Valerie.

I'm not saying that all grieving parents should immediately rush out and go to the nearest psychic. You firstly have to be in tune with the person, as I was with Valerie. She was placed in my life for specific reasons, as were others when it was time for me to meet them. What I am saying is that we cannot die! Your loved ones are still there; they know what you are thinking, they know what you are feeling, and still wish to remain a part of your life so talk to them, write out your feelings about them, they will know.

By all means search for a psychic if you wish,
but keep trying until you come across one that is
centred in love based spirituality. You will soon
know by what you are told that you have or have
not got someone that is connected with your loved
one. The truth will be self evident to you. You are
connected through your hearts and it is your heart
that will tell you there is no stronger bond in all
the universe. Even across other dimensions, love
is what binds all planes of existence together. And
also what causes some loved ones to volunteer to
come here only to die, and even then only because
they love you and you required that experience for
your own evolution.

During my learning experiences with my Master
it became apparent that her main objective on earth
was, given the approach of the much heralded 2012,
to show people what has to be done to complete their
time on earth and pay back all their karmic debt in
order to be free to then begin much higher learning
in other planes of existence.

For a long time getting off the earth permanently
was my only concern. I did not wish to remain in a
place where there was a chance that such pain and

anxiety and terror that I had just been through could occur again. But something that Valerie said during one of my many visits to her really caused me stop and think again.

My own Taryn, during her past life was herself a healer and this explained so much for me. Her comment about having to 'Take the good with the bad' on earth spoke to my awareness of a much higher spiritual evolution than my own, that together with her volunteering to return and endure all that suffering, for my benefit, and also to eliminate much of her own karmic debt made me begin to understand the extent of the love that is available for us all in our real home.

Shakespeare was so correct in his summation of the earth being merely a stage and our roles being nothing more than our current lives. That and the fact that her love drew her to me every night to help heal the wounds I still suffered in my relationship with my mother.

I began to think that I could do no less than, by way of honoring my loving daughter,than following Valerie's advice and learning to be a healer myself. Valerie was right; there were times when she had held my hand to strengthen our connection that she could feel the strength of the energy within me and after my own meditation I had often noticed many times what had appeared to be steam, or at times purple light being emitted from the palms of my hands. So I made the decision to allow Valerie, a Master of healing herself, to teach me the art of Reiki, and become a channel for the Chi (or Ki in Japanese) form of healing which originated in Tibet.

By this time though, I fortunately received a sign from my guides that I had seen the effects of my parents damaging conditioning and had gained great value from the lesson, so it was time for me to leave them and live on my own again. I needed to remove myself from the negative thinking now that I had learned the lesson.

Since my separation from my wife, I had felt great compassion for Darce, my father in law. Susan did her best to be a dutiful daughter but their relationship remained complex. Darce had a form of Pagets disease and had pain most of the time from his own hip. I grew to love Darce and we became good mates. I used to visit and eat with him quite often, which he clearly appreciated and our bond grew much stronger.

I called Susan after I had visited Valerie and told her that we could communicate with our Taz in this way, but her lack of belief in God got in the way and she feared to take advantage of the situation much to my dismay. This was and is a view I will never understand.

But we are all called to live our own lives in our own way. She grieved and loved in her way and I grieved and loved in my way.

In reality Susan no longer wished to see me. Susan, during one of my Leah's trips back to Australia had made it clear via Leah that she didn't want me to contact her or have much to do with me. I did find this hurtful but it was an ego response. We were at different places on different paths.

No doubt my developing relationship with her father was also difficult for her given the very different one that she had with him. Perhaps it was why Susan did not let me know when he passed away. I was visiting Eino in Taree, looking after his property while he was away when it happened.

I cried when I found out by way of a phone call from my mother. I loved Darce and this was a huge loss for me. I quickly hurried back to see if I could help with the arrangements at Darce's house, but as soon as I got there I was asked to leave.

After things settled down Valerie had constantly asked when I was able to begin learning her healing and I thank her for her persistence. There came a time where she needed to come to Sydney to teach a younger girl who also wanted to learn, so I thought that was an ideal time to begin to learn myself.

After learning of the history of the methods used and honouring the ancient healing Masters a Reiki Master will then, with her own higher level of energy open up the hand and crown charkas and the energy will begin to flow through your body. Much meditation is necessary but after you become a channel for the healing energy, whenever you call it to you, this process then becomes a permanent fixture within you for the rest of your life.

Three significant events occurred on that day. The first was that Taz was there to observe and honour my efforts. Once, while up at Valerie's she had run her finger across the side of my temple creating an itch of sorts, one that I found necessary to scratch a little. Valerie being at that point able to see more than I could told me that it had been my daughter being in a playful mood.

Taz was also there on the day I became a healer and let me know by repeating the same itch on my temple. This was her way of letting me know that I had her blessing. Then while Valerie's final initiation into Reiki was being performed she informed me that several visitors had made an appearance at that time. My own Master had come, to ensure that I was protected during the process and then arrived some Tibetan monks who had come to again honour the dedication I had just made to healing.

In addition my Taz had been so pleased at my commitment to healing that she honoured me with a hug and rested her head on my shoulder. I was so grateful on that day for taking the initiation in Thailand all those years ago because my Master had assured that along with my Taz, Olive her grandmother and Darce her grandfather, who I had missed terribly had all turned up at the same time to honour the commitment I had made and that had told me that they were all safe and in the best of hands.

That was the day I started to work for the divine. Reiki energy really does work to heal the body. If there are any illnesses or trouble spots about to occur in a person, a practitioner with feel the warning signs since they first occur in the aura, months before anything is evident in the body itself and there can be great value in this.

Chapter Nine

ENERGY TRANSMISSION

For many years I could not understand why England held such an attraction for Leah. It baffled me. Every time she was home here I was always trying to get her to remain, but it wasn't to be.

After Taryn's funeral she rushed back to England. It would be some time before I had a better understanding of the draw that England had upon her.

In time she confided that she had walked past a building in London and without ever entering the place knew precisely what was inside. Leah had spent many past lives in England and I knew at that point why her need was appearing to be so urgent; there were many people in London with which she had karma to work out. I miss her terribly and can only hope that she will return to us in the future.

I will say however that Leah and my son Dane both arrived on earth with an intuitive knowledge that there were much greater truths to the universe than were offered by organised religion and hopefully I have assisted to some degree in their own search for what their truth is.

Mankind passes through three stages.

First he worships anything: man, woman, money, children, and earth and stones.

Then, when he has progressed a little further, he worships God.

Finally he does not say: 'I worship God'; nor 'I do not worship God.'

He has passed through the first two stages into the last.

He knows beyond all doubt that there is no separation between God and himself.

Rumi

It has occurred to me many times that life, for a significant portion of the population, remains no more than a collection of habits. Organised religion has largely fallen by the wayside. Some people will blindly engage in the empty rituals and all the hollow phrases out of habit but the truth has mostly been withheld as was evidenced by the information discovered within the dead sea scrolls and other significant pieces found in Egypt. For some obscure reason church elders in the past found that we were more easily controlled if we feared God and that we existed as entities that were separate from the divine; that we had to earn our right to enter God's kingdom by behaving in a certain manner.

There never were Ten Commandments; I live by five only, the precepts required by any Master that has ever been on the earth. God has given us the freedom to behave in any fashion that we choose and many of us have done just that, but in doing so, the further we moved away from what God was the harder we made it for ourselves to return to what we actually were; to discover within us the bottomless well of love that we truly are. All evil that exists on the earth, and in the adjacent dimensions of the astral plane and in certain dimensions likened to hell, can only have been created by negative thoughts and energy arising from human beings whilst on earth.

We have the ability to create both the best and the worst that can exist in the entire universe, yet we spend our time, thoughts and energy trying to survive in the world in which we live. Questing after power or money or sex, we have been so conditioned that we are no longer able to be at peace. We rush around everywhere and we have been convinced that there is never enough time to do what we have to do every day. It is never more obvious than on our roads that manners have fallen by the wayside and selfishness prevails.

Fears occupy a great deal of our thoughts each day but we aren't 'present' enough to be able to be aware of them; we are not in tune enough to be able to monitor our thoughts sufficiently.

There is no 'luck' either good or bad, there is only either a positive or negatively charged thought, emotion or action. We create everything that happens to us, mind you, as I've hinted some events are the result of experiences required for the current life's evolution. But our fears cause many an unhappy experience for most of us. It is not until after some time is spent in meditation that one could develop an ability to begin to monitor our internal thought dialogue and to respect the effect that our thoughts, words and actions have on the world around us.

People seem to be under the impression that we are still living on the same earth that we grew up on; we are not. The earth is being immersed in a photon belt. These particles of light that surround us have the effect of raising the rate at which we and the entire planet vibrates. This is the cycle that is hinted at and referred to as 'The new age.' It is a cycle that regularly occurs, a golden age, an age of reconnecting with source. But at the moment people brought up without a higher consciousness, without a spiritual awareness, or the knowledge of anything outside of himself or herself, or God in other words are viewing life as a battle, a struggle, and as a result treat other people as obstacles or enemies that represent a competitor.

This is why people are appearing to be more selfish on our roads; if you view life as a battle that is what you will create, you create your own struggle with your very own thoughts. There is only you, everything that happens to you comes from you.

People, after experiencing many lifetimes of the inherent emptiness of what passes for religion no longer will tolerate a watered down meaningless ritual. What we are heading for is an age as was experienced by the most ancient Egyptians where the absolute truth was known by all; where direct contact with God was possible and commonplace.

It is no accident that in the past the church elders thought it necessary to heavily edit the texts. They do not want people to be able to contact God directly, hence there was no mention of reincarnation being left in the texts, there was no mention of meditation being a necessary requirement of connecting to God or your guides. They wanted us to fear God, they wanted us to feel that we are separate from God and have to earn our way into heaven. It is laughable the extent of the manipulation of the original texts. Our souls are literally a portion of God, how can we ever be separate from our source, and in fact separate from the source of all things; we cannot.

We are moving into a time of great expansion, a time where our heart is going to be our only guide to show us the way forward, where love will be the only emotion necessary to survive. Some people will find it difficult to adjust or perhaps to survive . The only thing that matters is how you treat other people; it is the only thing that has ever mattered.

It has been said that knowledge is power, but just suppose
For a moment that power were knowledge, that might just be
Of real significance on the earth.

Science will eventually come to a point where it will be understood that the space between all the atoms that comprise the entire universe is God; there is nothing else.

But life after life we are again placed within the earth with only a vague recollection of why we are here, adrift among a thousand distractions and pursuits that appear limitless. Fortunately God is in no hurry. In the end there is nowhere else to go, except back to our source.

The honour of a man is in his learning.
Wisdom is a torch lighting the path to
the truth. In knowledge only lies man's
opportunity for immortality. While a man's
body may die, it is only his wisdom that
he carries that has the possibility of living
eternally and continuing to grow.

Our task in this world is to learn and to grow. Those who do not will continue to repeat the painful journey of life through this world in body after body after body. Until we do learn. We are called to 'wake' so that we may 'see' the truth and rise higher upon our spiritual path.

It is mentioned more than once in the bible 'awake' – 'sleep not' and even Christ's disciples slept while Jesus prayed and meditated in the garden of Gethsemane for the last time. We have been told since the beginning of time that our waking slumber is far more dangerous than that which we experience at night. Men have always assumed that these terms from the bible are just a figure of speech, a metaphor, they could not be more wrong.

Our possibilities are very great; you cannot believe even a shadow of what humanity is capable of attaining. But not in sleep. Within the consciousness of a sleeping man or woman illusions and dreams are mixed with reality.

Most live out their lives unaware of the potential power that they possess. It is knowledge which leads to states of higher consciousness and that takes first awareness and then serious work.

I relate the following story that was published by some other initiates of the Master that my soul is permanently joined with. I remind you that one of the prerequisites of initiation is that you may not lie in any form, for any reason.

One day while they were out, some thieves decided that they would rob the home of the initiates. The power of a Master is such that many cannot fathom that a human being can attain such heights but it was later discovered that after the thieves were in custody on another matter it was found that while they were in the home of the initiates the television turned on and a tape of one of the Masters many teaching lessons began to play.

After watching for some time the thieves were apparently moved by the Master's words and decided that they would not touch anything in that home. When the initiates returned home later the whole story was related to them by the police. The initiates were quite relieved that they had been left untouched, but upon further examination they checked in their tape machine and found it empty of any tapes whatsoever. Any Master is in possession of abilities that appear to be unbelievable to anyone in the 'sleeping' world and the degree of protection that an initiation can afford one.

'Choosing'
(The search for fulfilment through meditation)

Choosing is the emptying of the heart of all things other than the search

For completion: this resembles a visualization that the body is empty, and that all thoughts have left it for a moment, that which can be called true thoughts will then flood in.

Hujwiri

The Masters that have come to the earth did so to have an effect on certain communities, at a certain time, a time when the community needed to hear those words.

> *Right time, right place, right people, equals success.*
>
> *Wrong time, wrong place, wrong people, equals most of the real human story.*
>
> Idries Shah

Because of the difficulty of maintaining the 'science' of man and his preponderance for living in a walking sleep state, religion is no longer a means of approaching any truth. It remains a vehicle in my mind but not one which takes us to the real truths.

In many forms of worship now human habits have ensured that prayer became no more than an endless repetition of the words at a given cue or prompting. People now only think that they are praying. Even if a prayer is repeated ten thousand times a day the mind will be wondering how long this will take, or what is for dinner, or why someone earns or has more than they do.

Mere repetition of words, in a religious sense is of no value. Each of the words must be reflected upon and the meaning must be understood. It must be felt in every cell of your body.

How many are capable of unconditional love for others?

Not as many as you would think. They may make a sufficient effort vocally and even monetarily when in a public arena, but the contents of many hearts rarely see the light of day. True feelings are often withheld; such is the difficulty in telling the truth all of the time. This is impossible for most of the human race that tend to make most of their decisions with their ego.

In so many cases prayer as we know it is no more than a petition before God for a better life or more money or any number of other things that people they feel they are lacking in life.

Many are of the belief that God exists but how many know what God actually is?

There can only be one answer to that question, God is a consciousness, a consciousness that is self-aware, but one that is unable to perceive itself. I firmly believe that gender can never be assigned to a being such as this. So in order to know itself our souls were created and are literally portions of the being we know as God with the same creative abilities. It was only in this way that the being could know itself, from a viewpoint outside of itself.

After much time spent in meditative pursuits and reading the associated literature one will ultimately as I did, come to a realisation that *'There is only you.'*

Everything that happens to you is caused by you, whether chosen consciously before you enter this world or chosen, usually unconsciously once you are here. Clearly, as I have said there are some events in your life that need to be experienced by your soul and those you cannot escape and must endure but there is much that you experience that arises from your own negative thoughts feelings and conditioning.

The following is perhaps a teaching story or fable that is used by the Sufi's as a tool of delineation of things that occur in real life or in a community, or in the mental processes of the individual. It comes from a book 'Reflections' compiled by Idries Shah.

PERCEPTION AND OBJECTIVE TRUTH IN RELIGION

Suppose no human being could tell hot from cold.

People would then not be able to make use of heat or cold. They would be at its mercy.

They would find that water sometimes scalded them, sometimes was nice and drinkable. Why this should be and how they could avoid dangerous water and select good water might become a ceaseless search. While they were searching, the behaviour of water — and a good many other things — would make no sense: it would seem to be motivated by some capricious fate. As has been seen in the past people would become superstitious about it, and would be attracted to anyone who could tell them something about it, or who seemed able to do so.

The fact would be, however, that they lacked an organ of higher perceptions, nerves which

*could signal to them when there was heat and
when cold.*

*They would be likely to be in such a
permanent state that they would actually
conflict with anyone who told them this,
though; because it would seem so trite. It
would also seem patronising. And, alternating
with their credulity towards 'teachers' of the
hot-cold problem would be a demand to be
'shown' evidences indicating what was going
on.*

*Someone might say, as we do, that the first
necessity is to develop the perceptive organ,
and that any residual argument, which
was left, could come later. But the vicious
circle would still be there: 'Tell me now,
demonstrate it now.'*

*Again since the organ of touch involved in
distinguishing heat from cold is specific and
cannot easily be described even to someone
who has other senses, a lot of time and effort
is wasted.*

*People think that they can be told what
'touch' is like.*

*When it comes right down to it, they can
only experience it. Speech, merely provides a
second rate guide to the actual possession of
the required organ.*

After my many years of meditation I have had
continued proofs that the divine is real and ever
present. Higher organs of perception and the proofs
that one receives once these organs are active cannot
be discounted or disputed.

There is no access to the divine by way of
prayer alone. A person with the purest of hearts
may achieve some success through prayer but it
cannot be overstated that meditation is 'two way
communication' with the divine, and no amount of
prayer will stop a loved one 'dying' if that is what
has been written by the soul in question.

It is the only way to God, Jesus and the apostles
and every other Master that has come to earth have
all taught meditation, there is no other way to
connect to the divine. The parables that appear in
the remaining texts, the ones that haven't been edited,

are not fully understood by many of the clergy, that much is obvious.

Spiritual Mastery comes only after many years of meditation prayer and study. Human beings, including some members of the clergy, are only able to understand more basic parables, teaching metaphors, or allegorical tales, to the level of their own comprehension. A serious student of the divine (one who does meditate) will find that as the years progress and if their Master is a real Master, that there are many layers to these stories. Some only become obvious to a reader after they reach a higher level of awareness, some stories may even contain several levels of significance. In many cases I've observed a sermon will centre on the most obvious meaning only.

Halls and theological colleges and learned
lectures, circles and cloisters –
What use are they when there is no real
knowledge within and there is no eye that
sees?

Hafiz

It is not fully understood that the Hans
Christian Anderson story of the Pied Piper of
Hamelin was originally a Sufi teaching story, one
of a township that, after refusing to pay the agreed
amount to the piper, lost to the piper, all of the
children of the village. This particular tale refers
to the extent to which humans give up their rights
to access any higher faculties in the endless quest
for more money. I live my life now only for these
higher faculties and so do many others. Man's
refinement is the only goal. In the origins of all
the faiths this was originally the only aim. It is
with great sadness that I observe the emptiness of
the world at large.

When I was initiated to my own Master it was
revealed that when she was younger she travelled
extensively throughout India, Asia and even high in
the Himalayas to search for the quickest method of
meditation which would enable a human to leave
the earth on a permanent basis (or achieve a level
of Mastery).

The method adopted was called the light and
sound method. During this type of meditation, firstly
a period is spent meditating on certain words, during

which light is sent from the divine and absorbed by your body; secondly a period is spent during which one would concentrate on a sound that emanates from other dimensions, this sound is often referred to as 'The Word.'

As typified by the quotation 'In the beginning there was the word, then the word was with God and then the word was God'.

This is a sound that is often described as the sound of a distant waterfall, a very powerful waterfall and is attributed with having the ability to clean out any impurities from the body.

During this meditation it is customary to cover your head with a piece of cloth. The top of the head is considered in many religions to be the most powerful place but perhaps a head covering also helped to disguise from those who might be watching, what was happening A crouched position is necessary to open the base Chakra and receive energy from the earth itself.

I believe there are links with the story of Moses when he climbed the mountain to speak with God indicate that he was meditating. Not that this is a story you will find in Christianity.

This covering of the head is something the Catholic church once demanded of women, indicating of course a common source for all religions. The turbans found in India and throughout the Middle East, the skull caps worn by Jews, the commonality of head coverings in religions is an indication that once they were all one. Or at least they have come from the same source.

Chapter Ten

WHAT IS REALITY?

Everywhere I look I encounter many who are apparently quite happy and content to accept the earth as it is. They have their goals, their dreams and their hopes for the future and they plod along with their own particular 'drug' of choice to mask their veiled insecurities.

There is no one on earth who is not insecure in some way and there never will be. The earth is not designed to allow for anything different. Perfection can only be achieved from a place of imperfection. Sadly, all too often, we only arrive at a place where we desire perfection because we have broken every rule there is to break. After centuries of doing anything we want, of killing, hurting others, of ignoring nature and the natural flow of things, of hurting ourselves and of ignoring God we shall, as I have, arrive at a place of impasse.

A place where a person does not know what they want from the earth, they don't know who they are, or even what they want to do on earth. They arrive at a place of, or a place near, completion. They have been on earth and done all there is to do, they have played every part in the play, taken on every role, sometimes a peasant at other times a king, smiled every smile, cried every tear, loved every type of love, and fought in every battle that can be fought.

What I write here is for those people. Don't misunderstand me. When I was younger I was no angel, but somehow I found the answer, I found the truth, and I write for all those that, like me, have been here since the beginning and need to know that there is a way out, that there is a purpose to the whole thing, and there is a love in existence, a love that is greater than anything that can be experienced on earth.

If it was not against the rules I would have left the earth long ago to rejoin my daughter, but apparently it is against the rules. So here I am. Ending our life solves nothing and may in fact create problems for us in the next world. We cannot escape and suicide is an attempt to escape. We will be sent back to undergo the same conditions again until they are able to find the inner strength (In their soul) to endure the same situation. There is no avoiding the will of God.

To all those who are still lost in the diversions of the earth I wish you luck, and a safe journey, but in the end, at some point, every single person on the earth will arrive at the same position I found myself in. You will go searching for the truth and for the way out of the cycle. But the way out is not as simple as it might at first appear. If you are quite content to reincarnate back here at the start of each new life consider this, why are there so many elderly people on the earth that have in fact such great difficulty in moving about without a walking frame, or some type of device to assist them? We pay a price at the physical level for our lack of spiritual development.

The process of life on earth, because of the distractions and diversions found here has a tendency to deaden our senses, to dull our awareness of all things that are not concerned with our day to day living.

Many people have been so mechanised they are no longer able to connect with the truth of our reality.

We are only aware of what is happening outside of ourselves; we have lost our connection to our inner selves.

Many times during my period of learning I have woken at night and found I am unable to move any part of my body. This on the face of it may be quite a frightening experience, but I slowly became aware that our souls, travel back to our home at night when we sleep, to recharge themselves. How can we be so far out of contact with the only part of us that is real? And the only part of us that is indestructible.

Our souls are our life and yet we are so far out of touch with our inner wisdom and we pay a price for that at the physical level, that many in the medical profession make quite a good living fitting us with replacement parts. So the process continues ad infinitum, we keep coming back here, we make the same mistakes life after life without the barest hint of any growth evident, lost in a maze of forgetfulness and the illusion of a seemingly fulfilling life which many are unable to cope with without their drug of choice. Life for many could not be more empty.

As I have already mentioned, my Master has insisted on her followers becoming vegetarian and living by the five Buddhist precepts. This I undertake without question. The benefits are undeniable as far as I am concerned and it is no accident that the Buddhists are vegetarian as well.

Meat is believed to slow us down at an energy level and those who are serious about the spiritual path wish to have levels of spiritual energy which are as high as possible.

I am not saying everyone has to do this but it works for me.

Chapter Eleven

WHERE ARE WE HEADED?

certainly don't expect that people will immediately drop what they are doing and begin a frantic search for enlightenment but there is no doubt that there are many that are in need of the truth.

I also know these words will resonate with those who are ready to begin such a search.

Many people seem lost and perhaps no more so than those of younger generations. There is a superficiality to life which creates emptiness and money, possessions, fame cannot fill that emptiness.

There have been many 'golden ages' on the earth, ages of spiritual awareness and real practices, practices that haven't been eroded by time and church elders that do not want us in direct contact with the divine or the absolute. If you want the truth, you must ask for it. If you ask in a clear fashion I have discovered that the divine will place the answer somewhere in your path. Listen to your inner voice, it will not blow around you like a gale, it will be a gentle whisper and that is your soul.

The most ancient Egyptians knew the truth, as did the Mayans and much information can be gleaned from 'The pyramid code' and the many other publications that have appeared in the last ten years. The truth is upon us right now and I have chosen to be part of it. I now live in the light even though there is still darkness on earth.

There have been many Masters that have come to the earth, there always will be, they are needed by those that sense the inner calling that draws those that are ready to begin the journey to our real home as I was. Any serious student of spirit, of meditation, will already be aware of the fact that Jesus has already returned to the earth and has been here for more than fifty years, yet the various Christian denominations are totally unaware of that fact, we have paid quite a severe price for our beliefs in the empty rituals and hollow phrases that pass as the truth.

Jesus said he was coming back, nowhere does it say that he was coming back in the same body. If you seek the truth I would begin your search by looking for an 'Ocean of Love' somewhere on the earth.

In the end I eventually finished writing my film script and I have high hopes following advice from my guides that eventually the film will be made. It was written as a metaphor that described my own journey.

During the time I was writing the script, even before my daughter had left the earth, the divine used various methods to alert me to the directions my story should be taking, sometimes they sent the messages via psychics, two of which were that elements from ancient Egypt needed to be included; one was the ankh the symbol of eternal life, the other was Khonsu the falcon headed god often depicted in many hieroglyphics, so I then had to return to the beginning in order to include this material.

Then at a later point I was woken by a dream sent by my guides, a dream that I could not understand, so I got up and went to my book of symbols.

The moment I pulled the book off the shelf, another book, one immediately next to it fell open onto the floor. At that point I was already aware that there are there are no coincidences, so I sat and read the Sufi metaphor that lay before me. It was a significant time in my life.

THE GARDEN

Once upon a time, when the science and art of gardening was not yet well established among men, there was a Master gardener. In addition to knowing all the qualities of plants, their nutritious, medical and aesthetic values, he had been granted knowledge of the herb of longevity, and he lived for many hundreds of years.

In successive generations, he visited gardens and cultivated places throughout the world. In one place he planted a wonderful garden, and instructed the people in its upkeep and even in the theory of gardening. But, becoming accustomed to seeing some of the plants come up and flower every year, they soon forgot that others had to have their seeds collected, that some were propagated

*from cuttings, that some needed extra
watering, and so on. The result was that the
garden eventually became wild, and people
started to regard this as the best garden that
there could be.*

*After giving these people many chances
to learn, the gardener expelled them and
recruited another whole band of workers. He
warned them that if they did not keep the
garden in order, and study his methods, they
would suffer for it. They, in turn, forgot —
and, since they were lazy, tended only those
fruits and flowers which were easily reared
and allowed the others to die. Some of the
first trainees came back from time to time,
saying: 'You should do this, and that,'*

*But they drove them away, shouting: 'You
are the ones departing from the truth in this
matter.'*

*But the Master gardener persisted. He
made other gardens, wherever he could,
and yet none was ever perfect except the*

one which he himself tended with his chief assistants. As it became known that there were many gardens and even many methods of gardening, people from one garden would visit those of another, to approve, to criticize, or to argue. Books were written, assemblies of gardeners were held, gardeners arranged themselves in grades according to what they thought to be the right order of precedence.

As is the way of men the difficulty of the gardeners remains that they are too easily attracted by the superficial. They say: 'I like this flower,' and they want everyone else to like it as well. It may, in spite of its attraction or abundance, be a weed which is choking other plants which could provide medicines or food which the people and the garden need for their sustenance and permanency.

Among these gardeners are those who prefer plants of one single colour. These they may describe as 'good'. There are others who will

*only tend the plants, while refusing to care
about the paths or the gates, or even the
fences.*

*When at length, the ancient gardener
died, he left as his endowment the whole
knowledge of gardening, distributing it
among the people who would understand
in accordance with their capacities. So
the science as well as the art of gardening
remained as a scattered heritage in many
gardens and also in some records of them.*

*People who are brought up in one garden
or another generally have been so powerfully
instructed as to the merits or demerits of
how the inhabitants see things that they
are almost incapable – though they make
the effort – of realizing that they have to
return to the concept of 'garden'. At the best,
they generally only accept, reject, or suspend
judgement or look for what they imagine are
the common factors.*

From time to time true gardeners do arise.
Such is the abundance of the semi-gardens
that when they hear of real ones people say:
'Oh yes. You are talking about a garden such
as we already have, or we imagine.'

What they have and what they imagine are
both defective—

The real experts, who cannot reason with
the quasi-gardeners, associate for the most
part among themselves, putting into this or
that garden something from the total stock
which will enable it to maintain its vitality
to some extent.

They are often forced to masquerade, because
the people who want to learn from them
seldom know about the fact of gardening as an
art or science underlying everything that they
have heard before. So they ask questions like:

'How can I get a more beautiful flower on
these onions?'

The real gardeners may work with them because true gardens can sometimes be brought into being, for the benefit of all mankind. They do not last long, but it is only through them that the knowledge can be truly learnt and people can come to see what a garden really is.

From 'The way of the Sufis.' A book of teaching stories and metaphors compiled by Idries Shah.

From that point on it was clear to me that my work on earth was to work to lead people to the truth. Clearly the metaphor's purpose was to explain why organized religion for the most part, was diluted and lacking the original truths it no longer contains. It was no longer the whole truth of which the Masters spoke and meditation had certainly fallen by the way. The universe had ensured that my early working life in the film industry, that and the fact that my life has mostly been spent watching movies, gave me the ability to actually write the film which I called Mystic.

So after more than twenty years of research I wrote of all of the abilities of which the Masters were capable. Here I speak only of 'complete men and women' those that actually live the truth, men and women of category seven and eight, a complete human being in every sense of the word, who have achieved the highest levels of connection with the divine?

These people, if you walked past them on the street will appear no different to anyone else, but my experience has shown me that nothing is impossible; I have personally witnessed miracles performed by my own Master.

My purpose in writing 'Mystic' was to show people how the universe actually works. I am sure writing that film, as in writing this book, has had a cathartic influence upon me.

In my writing I see the opportunity to turn pain and terrible suffering into something worthwhile.

Chapter Twelve

OUR FEELINGS CAN BE QUITE POWERFUL

The journey that I am on has been a difficult one and may well remain so. It is for everyone although for some it is harder than others.

Ascension can be likened to fighting your way off the earth. There will be many battles that will confront you. You will just finish one battle and another part of your early conditioning will rise up to confront you yet again. You will need help, but in all fairness the universe will respond by placing the help somewhere in your path. The universe is on your side, it actually wants you to succeed, so don't hesitate to ask for help. Your guides will know what you are thinking and what you are feeling at any one time. They know it all. And be particularly aware of your dreams.

It is my fondest hope that most of you will not suffer the way I have, by the loss of a child. For many it will be as simple as addressing your fears, providing you are aware of what your fears are.

Some of mine were from a past life, some from me forming an erroneous opinion at an early age, others were inherited from relatives or peer groups. Most people have a fear of psychiatrists but it may be worth considering if you undertake this process because there will be times when you need support.

I saw one briefly after I had cancer, a good one. There are many of them, they may be of great value in identifying underlying fears of which you are not aware. A case in point for me was my being beheaded in a previous life and developing a fear of death, although perhaps a psychic would be more in order there, or a regression under hypnosis.

Hopefully some of you are not in such a devastating rush to leave the earth as I am, given the life I've had. I fully understand that it was my own soul that elected to undergo this life and these circumstances, as yours did your own life, but coming back to undergo perhaps similar events again, raises the question: 'What the hell for?'

If you are happy to take your time and begin the process over a few lifetimes, I wish you luck.

I suppose the most difficult thing to accept is that after plodding along through life thinking that you have some control of your life, there comes a time where it becomes blatantly obvious that you have no control whatsoever, over anything. I blindly kept walking through my life with only a whisper in my ear, a curiosity about how everything worked. But people began turning up at certain times that led me in certain directions, I guess it was not all that bad until I started meditating, after that, slowly but surely your guides will engineer your life to present your fears to you. This is necessary; fear cannot exist in higher dimensions.

In higher dimensions, it is possible to create many things, virtually anything you desire after you undergo a healing from the life you have just completed. But even after creating some type of perfection for yourself, perhaps after a century or two or three, time is relative to the space you are in, ultimately you will begin to long for a more complete knowledge of the full extent of existence and even of God, so you will elect to be back here to complete your evolution.

At this point I have been asked by my guides to mention two aspects of the process that become increasingly important as time goes on.

Valerie my own teacher was fond of saying to me; 'Honour yourself and you will be honoured.' After I had received the money from the sale of our house, I was a little complacent with my thoughts about money. I put it in the bank of course, but I do recall my cousin Diane remarking at one point that if your fear was great enough, they (Your guides), may end up taking everything you had. And that is exactly what happened. Which was enough to convince me how powerful our fears are. My fear of having no money, resulted many times in the complete loss of all of my work, the phone just stopped ringing.

This in effect, over a few years taught me two things, firstly that all our emotions create. In this universe cause and effect control everything. Within us there can only be 'love or fear' as underlying motivations; they are the two emotions that we emit that have the greatest potential to either bring us undone or lift our vibrations much higher. Fear will create a negative event in our lives the quickest and bring us undone without fail. The emotion that sits at the top of the list and is born of love is compassion. And if it is a closer position to the divine that you seek, along with meditation, compassion will raise your vibratory rate faster than anything else. Those who appear less fortunate than us, although their soul may have chosen those events, when we see them in need we must help if it is within our power.

And secondly it showed me that we have minimal control over the material world we are in. As a result of my fear, as time went on, I found myself spending as little on myself as possible, living on the bare minimum I could spend on either food or clothes. But thankfully I eventually got to a point where I began to listen to Valerie's words, since it appeared that nothing was going to change until I did. I did begin to honour myself and I began to find, little by little, that if you do buy the things that you need, and you do trust the universe, then the universe responds to that trust by allowing money to flow to you again; to make room for more money to flow to you, you have to let go of the money that you have.

Also within this particular lesson, is an issue of 'the inner child' within all of us. Life without 'fun' is not life at all, there has to be fun in your life. You should incorporate fun into the work you do and no one should be doing a job that they do not enjoy. There is not one person on earth that should not have incorporated fun into their very livelihood; it should not be a commodity that one can purchase after the end of a day's work.

Another thing to consider on this path is the issue of self-discipline. Human beings require self-discipline if we are to succeed in any direction. If we do not have discipline, firstly, various substances will take hold of us and dominate our lives. This is mainly due to becoming 'locked' in the lower chakra just beneath our navel, which controls the body itself and automatic functions.

Energy follows thought and where you focus your attention is where your energy will go. The best chakra to work with is the Sixth, the forehead, or third-eye chakra because this is the one which controls all the other charkas and holds the potential for the most power and wisdom.

But again it is wise before doing any work with chakras to do some reading and work out the best course for you.

For whatever reason when I was younger I never had a problem with discipline. Martial arts practice can sometimes be arduous and even painful, but I was never tempted to give up. So when it came time to meditate much later, I needed to find the answers to life to such an extent that some days even four hours of meditation presented no obstacle for me. There are some that say that it is not necessary to meditate for more than twenty minutes daily, but given the extent of our karmic debt, and the words of a Master twenty years of practice, for three hours a day, to achieve some form of total freedom I would suggest you do as much as you can cope with.

One other annoyance you may have to cope with may be your own ego. In the beginning; you will be constantly bombarded with thoughts from the ego, trying to unsettle you and get you to go and watch the television, or get something to eat or drink. This can be quite annoying but in time the ego will eventually quieten down. It will eventually see that you are serious in your efforts and will leave you alone because it will see that meditation is not work, which it hates. So whatever happens, just keep bringing yourself back to your efforts and look for your place of quiet within.

After I was initiated I lived in Terrey Hills, a suburb north of Sydney, an area surrounded by plentiful amounts of bushland. I found it convenient since I was unattached at that point, to walk into the bush to meditate.

I used to begin with one and a half hours in those days. I realize that not everyone is in a position to be near such a natural setting like this, but you should if at all possible, try to make an opportunity to do this when possible. But any meditation is better than none. I just found that being surrounded by trees, whilst sitting on a rock left me when finishing, with a most delightful feeling of floating, a quite otherworldly sensation.

When the ego finally leaves you alone and you begin to feel a peace within your body, you will usually find that you are making some headway and when you start to lose track of time this usually signifies a deeper level of concentration, please persevere.

During meditation two things occur, firstly energy flows into you from the divine, into the crown of the head centre, and secondly the earth itself reciprocates by energy flowing up into you via the base chakra as you sit. The entire universe acts as conductors that channel energy (Light) from the divine; all suns, planets and moons all serve their function in this process. In fact more than once I've been sent dreams from my guides about 'rocks,' this particular sign is letting you know that you are not grounded sufficiently, so occasionally if this sign appears sit on the earth, or walk in bare feet, energy from both these sources is necessary for our evolution, and for a balanced being, being disconnected from these energies for lengthy periods can do nothing but create illness within us.

Chapter Thirteen

YOU RECEIVE
WHAT YOU EMIT

Too many people stay in jobs they do not like, dreaming about escaping their lot. Many dream about a future time where all will be well, after 'this and that' event occurs and when these dreams do finally eventuate, all will fall into place and at that time happiness will finally be theirs; they will have 'arrived' and the world will be their oyster.

Of course underlying these dreams and impeding their fulfillment, are the subtle beliefs and early conditioning they have experienced. They must first, in their sub conscious, truly believe that they are worthy of success. In reality many do not or cannot. Hence the damage done by our parents can remain with us for all our lives.

If a young child is told many times that they are a naughty child, they will actually believe it. Or perhaps they are told they are 'stupid' or 'dumb'. All these words have an effect on the young. So it becomes an imperative that, as time goes on, you become aware of your feelings about yourself.

This requires learning to observe. The more you observe the more you know yourself; the more you know yourself the more you can master yourself and change yourself.

I say once more, there is no 'luck' either good or bad; every single thing that happens in your life stems from you, the ultimate cause being your inner beliefs about yourself, and the inner beliefs manifest by way of the energy that you emit. The thoughts, feelings and emotions that flow from you at every moment of the day are the things that create your reality and reflect what you believe about yourself.

When you become aware you learn to observe and when you observe you are able to direct thought consciously instead of thought unconsciously directing you as is so often the case.

Anyone who is not connected to the divine should endeavor to look into their inner beliefs and try to be aware of what they are thinking and feeling as the day goes by. The universe will send you whatever it is that you are emitting. A man stuck in an unappealing job, who tends to be emitting negative thoughts and feelings will get exactly those types of events occurring in his life. If a person wishes to be happier, that person must first decide to be happy in whatever they are doing now. If a person feels that they need more money in their life, they need to cultivate a feeling of being rich and not hesitate to spend the money that they already have.

The same applies to romance, or love, you must first emit love into the world before it will come back to you, this again can be related back to cause and effect. Whatever it is you feel you are lacking in your life you must cultivate the feeling of already having it, and then the universe will reciprocate.

More than thought it is the feeling, the emotion, which is the power. When thought is combined consciously with this power the effects are indeed miraculous.

Chapter Fourteen

ON LEAVING THE EARTH
AND OUR VERY FIRST VISIT

A new soul, arriving on earth for the first time, needs a period of adjustment, a time where not too much will be expected of them, so that they may get used to a human body.

Some arrive with greater handicaps than others. Those who are physically or mentally disabled clearly come into this world to do more challenging work than the rest of us. But in the main they are surrounded by those who can support and love them.

All of us come into this world to learn. And all of us leave this world when we have learned what we needed to learn.

As far as death goes there is more than adequate information available in the world to seriously consider the fact that we cannot die. Many have written about their own 'near death' experiences, especially those that were sent back here because their work was not yet complete. The most common accounts will relate a description of 'the tunnel' and our journey along the tunnel to its end, at the light.

Within our body there is an 'energetic' tube that links all our chakras or energy centres and will facilitate our exit from the body; this is the tunnel people speak of, the correct spiritual term being the 'transmigrational tunnel'. What happens at the end of the tunnel may vary, but usually, your own soul guides will greet you, or for some, it may be a relative that has had a particularly significant impact in the life you have just left.

I have asked that my daughter Taryn is the first person that I will see. A person will usually exit the body through the centre that they have used the most in their life; people who talk a lot will exit through the throat centre. Those who have been physically active and competitive in their life may exit through their naval centre, a loving person who has demonstrated much compassion in their life will exit through their heart centre.

After leaving the body, there exists for all of us, a dimension that reflects our actions and the rate at

which we have vibrated during our lives. The way
we have treated other people, or more pertinently,
how many people we have helped and how many
we have hurt. Although no one in the higher planes
will ever judge you, if you should enter the higher
planes, an integral part of the transition will be that
you will experience a comprehensive view of your
entire past life, during which you will experience all
the pain that you have caused other people, and it
may be, for some, a long overdue wake-up call.

The whole purpose of planetary life is a process
of awakening, of achieving. At this point I should
mention the spirits that are not ready to leave the
earth plane quite yet, otherwise known as ghosts and
there are a couple of variations in this category.

Some spirits become so deeply attached to things
of the earth that they refuse to go anywhere. Some
houses that are so deeply loved by the owners that
they remain and will not give it up, much to the
dismay of the next owners. Other spirits, after losing
a loved one, choose to remain in that place, hoping
for the return of their lover.

Another instance of ghosts is where people have
died in great pain and suffering and the emotional

stress is 'recorded' in the site of that suffering. Whether it is a building or a place, their pain will continue to exist in that place and may be picked up by people in the future... even centuries later. There is, in all truth, no solid matter, so that the pain and the emotion of that event actually becomes part of the building itself, and the situation replays itself indefinitely.

Yet another category of earthbound spirits is those that allow themselves to become addicted to the various substances found here. If a person's body becomes addicted to a substance, and if that need is all consuming, then ultimately, the body then needs it so badly that the very soul within it begins to vibrate at the same level as that substance. With the result that the soul, at the time of death, does not want to leave, it will then, in spirit form remain on earth and frequent all the regular venues where the substance was usually found. The souls of former alcoholics, once one has achieved the ability to see higher vibrational energy, can be seen at times in local hotels, hoping against all odds that without a body they can still achieve some contact with their precious liquid, but to no avail.

But in effect most of us will make the transition to what is referred to as the astral plane. This particular plane is known to exist with over one hundred different levels, each one of which has a vibratory rate slightly higher than the next. The lowest levels here are closely related to what the Christian churches would call purgatory. This is a realm, because it is so close to the earth plane in vibration, that contains much negativity and beings of negative intent. Living within this region are beings that anyone from earth may not be able to comprehend, these beings are a product of planets elsewhere in the universe. Humans of low or unpleasant vibratory levels or perhaps of ignorance will usually become trapped in these lower levels.

Also within these realms there are found certain demonic entities, these in particular are created purely from the negative thoughts and actions of human beings on earth, in this and past centuries. These beings who are more beasts than resembling any form of humanity, if they are given the opportunity, they are the ones that wait and will tend to prey on people of weak wills in order to enter their bodies and gain a foothold on the earth. They are also the beings that will; if someone happens to be out of their body in the astral planes will try to enter the body whilst the astral body is away.

There are many theories about what exists beyond this world but the important thing to remember is that the more you advance spiritually in this life, the better prepared you will be for whatever you encounter. And, just as you have angels and guides to help you while on earth so you will be helped when you pass over.

The majority of the people on earth think of death as something to be feared but this cannot be more of a fallacy. It is nothing more than us returning home. Let's face it, reincarnation being a fact, how many of you can remember any of your previous deaths? It is no more than a gentle separation from the body, painless, and often the soul begins its journey out of the body before any pain (as might be felt in a serious car accident) can occur.

Many people feel that heaven and all the other dimensions occur in some mysterious far off place, this also is incorrect. After years of meditation I am able to see many things, there is always much energy and higher vibrating beings all around us all the time. As I nod off to sleep every night, I can quite clearly see my own soul guides as they appear to tend to any healing that I may have needed from that day; all dimensions occupy the same space.

You just can't see them. If you could most of you would be overwhelmed. In actuality there is a level of the astral plane to suit everyone from the earth. The middle of the astral planes is where perhaps most people on earth will arrive; there will be a period of healing usually required for most of us.

Most levels of the astral appear to resemble earth, showing parks and buildings of varying types. In these levels we are still relatively handicapped, by having a brain, hence our beliefs about death and an afterlife take on great significance. A person of balance without significant fears should be able to create relative comfort for themselves there, but being accustomed to the physical world they tend to surround themselves with objects they are used to and many will appear to be happy for quite some time, perhaps even for a century or two.

This is why mastery of Self and mastery of mind is so important in this world. Meditation is a process which allows us to attain higher levels of that mastery.

But ultimately no matter what you create for yourself, after a period, an awareness descends that tells you that there is much more to existence than what you are experiencing. Some may, after becoming aware of the totality of the entirety of creation, elect to return to the earth to continue with their spiritual evolution, since the whole truth can only be available to a soul that has resolved all their karmic debt, and the fastest growth can only occur whilst in the earth plane in a human body. People that have shown much love in their lives will clearly end up in the higher levels of the astral, the process however is one of vibration only; you will automatically manifest at the level of your earthly vibration.

Those who in life have had a spiritual awareness can, as time and relativity pass climb a little higher in the astral. The result being that the particles that comprise their being slowly become finer and lighter. Growth or evolution in this region certainly is possible and souls can move into higher levels of the astral, but it takes a little longer than on earth. You would also be able to see many souls from past generations or significant figures from earth's history if that is your wish, as well as your lost relatives.

Communication is mostly telepathic in nature, and a pleasing surprise is the amount of freedom that we experience once we are free of the earthly body, which has often been compared to living within a damp sponge.

Once a soul ascends to the higher astral plane it will come into contact with what is referred to as the causal plane, this will be your first opportunity to connect with the Akashic record. In this area you will behold a type of three dimensional library containing the history of the entire universe and of every soul that ever was, whether from earth or any other planet. The Akashic record exists as a complete record of all that has ever been, a computer that stores a three dimensional experience of the entire universe. And every thought or emotion that has ever been experienced.

This place in itself is, in essence, an area that serves as a place of observation, it is accessible to beings of all other planes, but is neutral in its potential for accelerated growth for the soul. Above the astral plane in the causal plane, everything is reduced to its essence. Nothing is lost. Everything you are and will be has been retained. However, the manifestation of a body is no longer important. You will now be aware that you are a being of light. You will not necessarily have a bodily form, but become mostly light. Your consciousness will no longer need a form, you may however return to the astral plane and will don an astral body once more if you feel it is necessary.

These states of being are perhaps difficult to fully accept while we are in a body. What draws us onwards to the higher planes is a search for the divine manifestation of love to know completion. We will wish to merge with the infinite, to return to where we began. A point comes when you will leave the astral form and move upwardly fully into the causal planes. This in effect, can be thought of as a second death, where you relinquish your ego and astral body and move closer to a merging with all that is, definitely like a death and a new birth. The Causal Plane corresponds to the intellectual centre. The experience is centred around thought and belief, and how these create our reality. Thought on the causal plane can be described as just as real as something solid on the physical plane. In the normal cycle of evolution, it is in the higher astral plane that entities reunite with other portions of their soul before moving onto the causal plane. It is from this plane of existence that beings who channel their teachings to us, such as Seth and Archangel Michael can be found.

It would be quite a task to try and rationalize the next level above the causal. The Mental plane is a region of abstraction, of thoughts and ideas, which tend to manifest as real objects. Those who find themselves here could be traveling through and interacting with their own thoughts, or even the thoughts of others. The Mental plane is also divided as with the other levels. Since the Lower Mental Plane overlaps the Astral Plane, they can often be confused for one another. Time here can tend to be felt as distorted, possibly even to the point of non existence, and it is possible to see future or past events as easily as the present.

The upper limit of the Higher Mental Plane is also the limit of the awareness of the personal self and individuality as we know it, and so is also the limit of our more subtle bodies. The Mental Plane is harder to reach than the previous two, but nonetheless it is achievable during an Out-of-Body experience, with difficulty, traveling to and above the mental plane, is referred to as mental projection, but this type of Out-of-Body experience can be quite rare.

Some metaphysical schools, aware of the inherent dangers in this level, have resorted to the use of certain chemicals to specifically induce an apparent experience of the mental plane. The reason being that some things experienced in this level can be likened to an L.S.D. trip, and if the student is to not become addicted to the unreal sounds, music and colours experienced here, they must learn the discipline to remain adhered to their original objective which is a union with the source of all that is.

The fourth level above the earth plane, according to my own Master is described as a universe of darkness, devoid of light or any type of illumination that can show you the way forward, there is no indication of how to complete your journey to the fifth level of heaven. According to my Master, and I do not doubt it, there has only one soul that has ever completed the journey to the fifth level without being shown the way by a Master, that man was George Ivanovitch Gurdjieff, a man written of extensively by P.D. Ouspensky in his book 'In search of the

Miraculous'. Gurdjieff, a man taught by many Sufi Masters clearly by the time of his death must have achieved a state of Mastery himself.

Above the fourth level of heaven lies the fifth plane, this is the place where all the Masters reside. For any soul that has ever incarnated on a planet, this is the highest level attainable for us. The particles that comprise our souls, after an incarnation, are too coarse to go beyond the fifth level. Although there is more of the absolute higher than the fifth, these souls have never set foot on a planet at any time. As an example, there exists a group of beings of finer particles called the 'Council of Nine' that are charged by the absolute with the task of the evolution of entire planets. My Master assures me though that even on the fifth level of heaven there is no more that one could possibly desire and that ultimate perfection and total fulfillment are our rewards.

The total freedom of the fifth level remains an unattainable illusion for most of us, and on earth a struggle against the forces of light and dark or choices between right and wrong remains with us, as was the intention of the divine. Since the universe is built on the principle of seven; seven chakras, seven

notes in the musical scale, and seven levels of the
transmission of energy from the divine, to all suns,
then to all planets, then to all the various moons,
to our sun and then to the earth itself. Even our
moon acts as a receiver of energy from all organic
life on earth. It is not a coincidence that the ancient
Egyptians worshiped Ra the sun God; or in a more
pertinent vain, they understood that the sun is our
nearest manifestation of God the divine, they were
much more aware than we think. All the objects in
the universe are manifestations of the divine.

Chapter Fifteen

. . . . NOW?

now spend my time either as a Reiki healer in honour of my daughter, who was a healer herself in her past life, or as an alternative I run courses to let people know the truth of our existence here and in other dimensions.

Meditation requires much training and discipline. There are dimensions which are not as comfortable as others. You can get into trouble exploring lower dimensions and it is important to know what you are doing.

Now, after years of spiritual practice I have achieved a level of awareness that allows me to see my daughter. She comes to visit me every day and every evening and we are able to communicate. If you have lost someone dear to you do not fear, you will see them again. Sometimes loved ones will try to alert you to their presence by making your lights flicker or perhaps they might hide your car keys. In the beginning my psychic Valerie alerted me to the fact that Taz wanted me to continue to talk to her, they still like to be connected to you and to feel that they're part of the family. Love is a bond that cannot ever be broken. You are permanently connected by your hearts, so keep talking to them, they will hear you, and they know what you're thinking.

I consider myself fortunate in that my spiritual level allows me to hear my daughter's words within my own heart, so trust me, we cannot ever die, we will watch the end of this universe and be there for the birth of the next one; we are indestructible.

All in all I'd have to say that I'm a lucky man. The universe has assured that I was led to the whole truth as has my daughter. Or perhaps 'engineered' to the truth may be a more precise term. But truth is a relative term, and is dependent upon your ability to recognize it as truth. I took it upon myself to look within my heart. All your answers can be found there, without the cumbersome interference of the 'ego'. Living in the light is living in love's domain, your heart knows what is right, it always will.

The longest journey you will make in your
life is from
Your head to your heart.

Sioux saying

The earth at the moment, is not in the best of condition and each of us is to blame for placing it there. As I said all planets are conscious beings. The approaching 'golden age' has been foretold for centuries, yet we are still buying vehicles that deplete the oil reserves of the earth and we still treat the earth as our playground.

I saw a sign outside a church the other day and had to smile:

'HAVE YOU BEEN SAVED?
IF YOU DIED TONIGHT, WOULD YOU GO
TO HEAVEN?'

It demonstrates the lack of understanding amongst those that profess to guide us, and explain God to us. No one, can keep us out of heaven; we are part of all that is. Our souls are God. Nothing can stop us from going to our rightful home. Even the worst offenders will be ushered up eventually.

One particularly unfortunate habit I observe on the earth is the propensity of humans for judgment. If people are not judging other human beings, they will continually judge themselves as being 'not enough'. No one on earth has the right to judge others,

You cannot know why someone else has come to the earth, if they have come here to learn the pitfalls of drug addiction, which their soul would need for evolving and to die alone in the gutter somewhere, then that is what needs to happen.

Of course compassion dictates that we try to help them, but if that is what the soul needs to learn then it will inevitably occur. You don't know why people are here, passing judgment on others at the very least amounts to telling a lie, and will only lower your spiritual level and make your own journey that much longer. *Who is the wrong person to judge? You.*

Judging ourselves can also be a gigantic trap; your soul chose all the conditions that comprise your life, yet I observe many that are clearly unhappy with who they are. Some consider themselves too fat, some too short, some too poor, everything that is 'you', all that is your life has been chosen for a specific reason. When considering an upcoming incarnation, everything has its place; all of us arrive here with varying 'tools' with which our souls will gain the experiences that are required.

Some chose to be born with an ample supply of money in their family, others chose to be born with an undeniably beautiful body, some require a tool of excess weight, all of these are no accident and it is wrong to consider them as such, they are only tools, their only purpose is to produce experiences that are needed for the soul. The only reaction that is paramount is one of acceptance and of respect for you, regardless of what any community or any social norm may be expecting of you. Honour yourself and the soul that sits within, and listen for it.

Due to the way the divine has constructed planetary life, given the Yin-Yang requirement that the balance of the forces be maintained, life may be considered as a series of highs and lows; periods of positive events followed by periods of negative events. This existence must be endured somewhat, but once one seeks an escape from this process these effects may be lessened considerably. The events occurring in your life must not be judged either; you must cultivate an attitude of walking through life with positive energy balancing on one shoulder and negative energy balancing on the other.

Judging one energy as being better or worse than the other, one being good and one being bad has the effect of drawing its opposite force to you. You must cultivate an attitude of both the positive and negative energies having a right to exist in the universe, just as you yourself exist.

People today are in danger of drowning in information but because they have been indoctrinated into thinking that information is of use they tend to be quite willing to drown in it. Much knowledge is either ignored, discarded or opposed because it comes from a source that is not projected from an institution or educational facility that purports to be a source of 'higher learning' and people will discard the information if it is not projected in any form that does not match what is expected from an institution of this type.

A donkey, laden with many books remains no smarter, a man weighed down with this information, undigested information, that someone in a past age thought to be relevant about any particular subject, unfortunately still passes for wise. In order to digest food a man requires a stomach; no one enquires however whether a 'wise' man is prepared sufficiently enough by way of higher perceptions to know what truth really is when it appears.

There is much of the truth out in the world, but you must ask for it, before the universe, or your soul guides, will place it in front of you, but it will come. I found much truth in the words of the Sufis, that cannot be denied,

But also I discovered that certain pieces of information, that these days are repeated as God's truth came originally from the past, where the Masters arrived at certain times, and said certain things that were designed to act on the people of those times, and the understanding or the comprehension of those people of that time is many times not applicable to the times in which we find ourselves today.

The result being that our comprehension suffers, hence the lack of appeal and relevance within organized religion. I cannot speak for everyone of course but a Master will show you what you need to know, not what you 'want' to know. For example, a Master will tell you that to give is a divine act, an act born of compassion, but many that I've observed give in a public arena. Charity, all too often, creates a feeling of obligation within the receiver. If you give in this fashion, it tends to create within you an emotion; you have a need to feel happy about yourself. Giving, if it is recorded anywhere and the recipient becomes aware, a Master will tend to call this a selfish act. Give unconditionally and in secrecy.

I suppose the most important thing I have learned is that the only key to happiness lies in our completion, finding our true selves underneath all the conditioning, underneath all our habits, underneath all our crutches that we depend on to be able to like ourselves. Jesus was right, the kingdom of God lies within, it is not outside of ourselves it never has been, nor will it ever be. The door to our real selves is within, and so is the key to that door. No one outside yourself can get you home, certainly in the beginning you may need some guidance, but ultimately you will undertake a journey within, a most rewarding journey. My own Master often states that her job is not to save us, her job is to guide us to the point where our own inner Master, our higher selves, appear to lead us home, via the heart.

After my life, although it is not over yet, I'm left with a feeling of regret over my loss but the consolation of knowing that I will see her again. That there is a greater purpose to all things. I don't know what will happen next. I suspect I have much more work to do here, perhaps as John Lennon has done, a man who was clearly in contact with his soul, I will be able to create something of beauty through the connection to my soul. But I will be shown that when the time is right, God always wins and you cannot hurry heaven, of this much I'm certain. So I wait.

Whatever your problems are, there is a way out, and a love waiting that you cannot imagine. Die (meditate) a little each day, during which time, if you meditate deeply enough your soul takes the journey back to our real home, and it is at that point the strength that is your soul will begin to flow into you. Once you really understand what love is, nothing on earth can stop you.

A Sufi view of conditioned judgement from various collections of Idries Shah –

An ignorant man looked at a browsing camel.
He said to it: 'Your appearance is awry'.
'Why is this so?'

The camel replied: 'In judging the impression
made, you are attributing a fault to that
which shaped the form. Be aware of this!'

'Do not consider my crooked appearance a
fault'.

'Get away from me, by the shortest route. My
appearance is thus for function, for a reason.
The bow needs the bentness as well as the
straightness of the bowstring'.

'Fool, begone! , An Asses perception goes with
an Asses nature'.

- On some less relevant forms of unity as practised
  in the east –
  Many people try to avoid using the word 'I'
  to demonstrate humility. The consequence of
  this is to fixate them on the very concept of
  'I'.

They get the reverse of the effect originally intended.

What is important is to know which 'I' is involved in any act or statement. This comes only through the experience of the various 'I's that exist within us.

* On evolution –
Man (As he imagines himself to be), in general, is a possibility only, not a fact. For most people, the sort of man whom they imagine to exist, or assume themselves to be, does not yet exist.

* On the Sufi's choice to remain somewhat aloof from mainstream humanity –
Effort makes some great men famous.

Even greater effort enables other great men to remain unknown.

- On human thought processes –
  From time to time ponder whether you are
  unconsciously saying: 'Truth is what I happen
  to be thinking at this moment.'

- On the methods of Sufi teaching –
  Because of the difficulty of grasping the fact
  that 'intellectuals' through laziness, have
  decided to 'abolish' any learning that cannot
  be gained from books, that is not to say that
  it does not exist. It means that it just makes
  it more difficult to learn and teach, since the
  intellectuals have trained people not to look
  for it.

- On our mechanical existence –
  Sleep is the brother of death.

- On the world –
  Treat this world as I do, like a wayfarer; like
  a horseman
  Who stops in the shade of a tree for a time,
  and then moves on.

- On attachments –
  *It is your attachment to objects which makes
  you blind and deaf to truth.*

- On death (Meditation) –
  Die before your death.

  *The Rose of Baghdad
  (Clearly a Master)*

  *Abdul-Qadir, founder of the Qadiri Order of
  Sufi's figures in an incident which gave him
  his title of 'The Rose of Baghdad'. It is related
  that Baghdad was so full of mystical teachers
  that when Abdul Qadir arrived at the city
  it was decided to send him a message. The
  mystics therefore dispatched to him, at the
  city's outskirts, a vessel, full to the brim with
  water. The meaning was clear:*

  'The cup of Baghdad is full to the limit.'

  *Although it was winter and out of season,
  Abdul-Qadir produced a full blown rose,
  which he placed on top of the water, to*

*indicate both his extraordinary powers and
also that there was room for him.*

*When this sign was brought to them, the
assembly of mystics cried out: 'Abdul-Qadir
is our Rose,' and they hastened to usher him
into the city.*

Just as the rose in this Sufi story symbolises that
there is room for more and that miracles are real
so my daughter Taryn, was and is my 'rose' and
a symbol that things are not always as they seem
and more is possible than we have ever imagined....
simply because we have not yet learned to truly
imagine.

In my journey it is death which has taken me
closer to life than I have ever been and it is the
journey of life, toward death, which is the one we
are all called to take as spiritual beings.

The Rose was here before we were and a fossil
some 40 million years old attests to this fact. It has
been revered by human beings since ancient times
and still today is the most loved of all flowers.

The Rose is also a powerful symbol of love and has been since time immemorial. Within a world of 'thorns' the rose emerges, fragrant, beautiful and enduring. This is the gift my daughter Taryn, my Rose of Baghdad, has given to me.